America's Legendary Frontier Towns: T[
and Dodg[

By Charles Riv[

Deadwood in 1876

About Charles River Editors

Charles River Editors was founded by Harvard and MIT alumni to provide superior editing and original writing services, with the expertise to create digital content for publishers across a vast range of subject matter. In addition to providing original digital content for third party publishers, Charles River Editors republishes civilization's greatest literary works, bringing them to a new generation via ebooks.

Sign up here to receive updates about free books as we publish them, and visit Our Kindle Author Page to browse today's free promotions and our most recently published Kindle titles.

Introduction

1882 picture of Allen Street in Tombstone

Tombstone, Arizona

"The 26th of October, 1881, will always be marked as one of the crimson days in the annals of Tombstone, a day when blood flowed as water, and human life was held as a shuttle cock, a day to be remembered as witnessing the bloodiest and deadliest street fight that has ever occurred in this place, or probably in the Territory." – The *Tombstone Nugget*

The Wild West has made legends out of many men, but it has forged a lasting legacy for the city of Tombstone, Arizona, a frontier boomtown that has come to symbolize everything about the Old West. In many ways, Tombstone fit all the stereotypes associated with that era in American history. A dusty place on the outskirts of civilization, Tombstone brought together miners, cowboys, lawmen, saloons, gambling, brothels, and everything in between, creating an environment that was always colorful and occasionally fatal.

Those characteristics might not have distinguished Tombstone from other frontier outposts like Deadwood in the Dakotas, but some of the most famous legends of the West called Tombstone home for many years, most notably the Earp brothers and Doc Holliday. And ultimately, the relationships and rivalries forged by those men in Tombstone culminated in the legendary Gunfight at the O.K. Corral on October 26, 1881.

The West's most famous fight all but ensured that Tombstone would be the epicenter of Western lore, and as the city's population dwindled at the end of the 19th century, the allure of Tombstone as a tourist center took hold. Nearly half a million tourists flock to Tombstone each year, where they find a city that has cashed in on its legacy through careful preservation. Many of the historic buildings in Tombstone haven't changed much in the last 130 years, and visitors who come to the O.K. Corral or Boothill Cemetery can get an idea of what Tombstone was like in 1881.

America's Legendary Frontier Towns: The History of Tombstone, Deadwood, and Dodge City comprehensively covers the history of the city, profiles the people who called it home, and highlights the attractions and events that made it famous. Along with pictures of important people, places, and events, you will learn about Tombstone like never before.

Deadwood, South Dakota

1888 picture of Deadwood

"On Wednesday about 3 o'clock the report stated that J.B. Hickok (Wild Bill) was killed. On repairing to the hall of Nuttall and Mann, it was ascertained that the report was too true." – The *Black Hills Pioneer*

In 1874, General George Armstrong Custer led a troop over of 1,000 men to investigate reports of the discovery of gold on Lakota-Sioux land in the Black Hills. Sioux ownership of the land stemmed from the Treaty of Laramie in 1868, but the discovery of gold changed things for the United States. The mining town of Deadwood quickly sprung up as prospectors descended on the area, even though the federal government had ordered military troops to set up posts there to keep prospectors out. Men like Al Swearengen and Charlie Utter came to make fortunes one way or another, Calamity Jane amused and irritated the townspeople in equal measure, and the legendary Wild Bill Hickok was shot and killed in one of Deadwood's saloons while holding the "Dead Man's Hand" by "the coward McCall."

Wild Bill's death helped ensure Deadwood would be remembered as an important part of Western lore, but in many ways the Deadwood craze was over almost before it began. During the 19th century, Deadwood's population reached its peak in the 1880s with a population of just less than 4,000, and fires, mining, and the closing of the frontier all made sure the population never grew. Today, barely 1,000 call Deadwood home, and it remains more an object of curiosity and tourism than anything else.

America's Legendary Frontier Towns: The History of Tombstone, Deadwood, and Dodge City comprehensively covers the history of the city, profiles the people who called it home, and highlights the attractions and events that made it famous. Along with pictures of important people, places, and events, you will learn about Deadwood like never before.

Dodge City, Kansas

"Dodge City Town Company, Ford Co., Kansas. Inducements offered to actual settlers! Prospects of the town better than any other in the upper Arkansas Valley! Free Bridge across the Arkansas River! The town a little over one year old, and contains over seventy buildings! Good school, hotel, etc. AT & SF RR depot in town... Enquire of: R. M. Wright at Chas. Rath & Co. store or E. B. Kirk, Secy and Treas., Fort Dodge." *Dodge City Messenger*, June 25, 1874

The Wild West has made legends out of many men, but it has forged a lasting legacy for some of the frontier towns that hosted famous Western icons as well, and aside from Tombstone and Deadwood, no frontier town is better known than Dodge City, Kansas. In the immediate wake of the Civil War, a settlement originally developed around Fort Dodge, which had been built to protect against Indian attacks, and it became a favorite spot for the buffalo hunters on the Plains who were engaged in exterminating the bison to harm the Native American tribes.

By 1876, however, Dodge City had become a popular destination spot for cattle drives starting from as far south as Texas, earning itself the nickname "The Cowboy Capital of the World". With that, the town also came to symbolize everything about the Old West. Dodge City brought together cowboys, lawmen, saloons, gambling, brothels, and everything in between, creating an environment that was always colorful and occasionally fatal. Since Dodge City was on the frontier, it took awhile for the law to catch up to it; even as late as September 1876, a local paper noted, "The citizens of Dodge have organized a vigilance committee and last week the committee addressed the following pointed note to every gambler in the city; 'Sir: You are hereby notified to leave this city before 6 o'clock, a. m. of Sept. 17th, 1876, and not return here.'"

Lawmen finally became a fixture of Dodge City in the late 1870s, but as with so many other places in the West, the line between hero and villain was blurred; cowboy Pink Sims later wrote about Dodge City, "It was stated that the marshals were all pimps, gamblers and saloonkeepers. They had the cowboys disarmed, and with their teeth pulled they were harmless. If they got too bad or went and got a gun, they were cut down with shotguns." Dodge City's lawmen included some of the most famous men of the Wild West, including Bat Masterson and Wyatt Earp, who mixed it up in Dodge City as a deputy marshal several years before he was involved in the Gunfight at the O.K. Corral in Tombstone.

America's Legendary Frontier Towns: The History of Tombstone, Deadwood, and Dodge City comprehensively covers the history of the city, profiles the people who called it home, and highlights the attractions and events that made it famous. Along with pictures of important people, places, and events, you will learn about Dodge City like never before.

2008 Reenactment of the Gunfight at the O.K. Corral. Photo by James G. Howes

America's Legendary Frontier Towns: The History of Tombstone, Deadwood, and Dodge City

About Charles River Editors

Introduction

Dodge City

   Chapter 1: The Early Years of Dodge City

   Chapter 2: Dodge City's Law Enforcement

   Chapter 3: Dodge City Entertainment

   Chapter 4: The Dodge City War

   Chapter 5: A Cattle Town Dies and a Legend is Born

   Bibliography

Tombstone

   Chapter 1: The Birth of Tombstone

   Chapter 2: People and Businesses Come to Tombstone

   Chapter 3: Tombstone Becomes a Town

   Chapter 4: Entertainment

   Chapter 5: Tombstone's Chinese Heritage

   Chapter 6: The Gunfight at the O.K. Corral

   Chapter 7: Revenge

- Chapter 8: The End of Tombstone's Glory Years
- Chapter 9: The Legends and Legacy
- Bibliography

Deadwood
- Chapter 1: The Birth of Deadwood
- Chapter 2: Wild Bill, Calamity Jane, and the Summer of 1876
- Chapter 3: Deadwood Takes Shape
- Chapter 4: The Fire of 1879
- Chapter 5: Al Swearengen and the Gem
- Chapter 6: Entertainment in Deadwood
- Chapter 7: Chinese Immigrants in Deadwood
- Chapter 8: The Decline and Rebirth of Deadwood
- Online Resources
- Bibliography

Dodge City

Buffalo hunter Charles Rath sits in Robert Wright's hide yard in Dodge City, 1878

Chapter 1: The Early Years of Dodge City

Before it ever occurred to anyone that the buffalo herds roaming the Plains were not unlimited, Dodge City looked for all the world like it would be Buffalo City, Kansas. Had it not been for the fact that a Buffalo, Kansas already existed, the small town that sprung up in the unforgiving terrain of the High Plains of southwest Kansas may very well have not been named Dodge City. Instead, the town that developed along the Arkansas River took its name from Fort Dodge, no more than 5 miles southeast from where Henry L. Sitler built a sod house near a cottonwood tree in the summer of 1872. The fort had been built to provide some protection from Indian raids as settlers made their way west along the Santa Fe Trail, and it was just one in a series of forts in the region meant to protect travelers. An earlier fort, Fort Mann, had been subdued by Indian attacks in 1848, and nearby Fort Atkinson had been abandoned by U.S. soldiers, so it would be an understatement to say the area was volatile.

Fort Dodge, Kansas

Sitler was a Pennsylvania native and a Union cavalry veteran who found himself a Confederate prisoner of war during the war. He was released in a prisoner exchange after William Tecumseh Sherman's "March to the Sea" destroyed parts of Georgia in 1864, and like many war veterans, Sitler drifted west. He spent some time as a buffalo hunter before setting up his ranch near Fort Dodge and contracting with the Army to supply the fort with hay. The "soddy" that Sitler built on his ranch has been given the distinction of being the first structure in Dodge City.

Dodge City may have started with one man and one structure, but Sitler was not alone for long. Acting on a rumor that a town was going to be built near the fort, a Canadian named George M. Hoover and his business partner, John G. McDonald, arrived in June 1872. By June 17, they had pitched a large tent, piled some stacks of sod blocks to serve as a bar, and opened the first business in what would become Dodge City. It is fitting that the first business establishment in town was a saloon, since the selling of liquor would become integral to Dodge City politics and play a part in so many of the town's most notorious episodes. Conveniently, the little outpost was just outside the reach of U.S. Army regulations and the ban on alcohol at Fort Dodge, and even when prohibition became law in Kansas in 1881 (and remained in place until 1948), that did little to slow the flow of whiskey in Dodge City.

The rumor that brought Hoover and McDonald to "Buffalo City" was true; the Atchison, Topeka, & Santa Fe (AT&SF) was in fact planning to build the railroad past Fort Dodge and on to Colorado, and the railroad's deadline was Christmas 1873. Soon after the town's first saloon opened, two men who had been contracted by the railroad to grade the land opened a general store south of the proposed line. These contractors ended up subcontracting out most of the work to brothers from Canada with the last name of Masterson, and their link to Dodge City history would go well beyond preparing for the arrival of the railroad.

Word of the impending railroad also spread among the buffalo hunters. George O. Smith and J.B. Edwards built a wooden shack near the 24-hour saloon and did brisk business selling groceries and other supplies to the hunters, and a second saloon soon followed that, built by

George "Hoodoo" Brown. A Frenchman named Frederick Zimmerman added a gunshop to the mix and he too had no shortage of customers. Estimates were that he sold anywhere between 50-75 guns a month.

Alberto Alonzo Robinson, recently promoted chief engineer of the AT&SF, also arrived around this time. Railroads wanted their depots in towns and took a hands-on approach to laying out the townsite plats, requiring at least some officials in the vicinity. Despite some troubles with horse thieves along the construction site, the AT&SF tracks reached Dodge City, 366 miles west of Atchison, by September 5, 1872 and within another week, tracks were laid 10 miles beyond Fort Dodge. The *Leavenworth Daily Commercial* reported of the town days later, "The 'City' consists of about a dozen frame houses and about two dozen tents, besides a few adobe houses. The town contains several stores, a gunsmith's establishment, and a barbershop. Nearly every building has out the sign, in large letters, Saloon."[1] Trains began to include Dodge City on their routes on October 7.

Although the little outpost had been nicknamed "Buffalo City", buffalo hunters had nearly wiped out the buffalo by the time the AT&SF reached Dodge City. Some were killed for their hide, but many were also killed for sport, bringing the animal to the brink of extinction after nearly 40 million buffalo roamed the Plains just two or three decades earlier. The express aim was to ensure the nomadic Native American tribes on the Great Plains could no longer rely on the animal, but it also had the effect of opening the door for a new commodity: cattle.

---

[1]Joseph W. Snell and Don W. Wilson, "The Birth of the Atchison, Topeka, and Santa Fe," *Kansas Historical Quarterly,* http://www.kshs.org/p/kansas-historical-quart...atchison-topeka-and-santa-fe-railroad-2/13188

The Longhorn Statue on Front Street in Dodge City today

The story of Dodge City may have begun with buffalo and the railroad, but the origins of the town as it's imagined today truly start with Texas. Around the time that the Civil War ended in 1865, the open ranges of south Texas were full of the cattle, known as longhorns. Hundreds of thousands of the distinctive steer, with their horns spanning as much as seven feet from tip to tip, roamed free on the range, so cattle ranchers took advantage of the bounty and claimed the wild longhorns as their own. With a beef shortage on the East Coast, the demand for cattle was high, so the ranchers just needed to get the cattle north from Texas to the nearest railroad.

Tennessee native Jesse Chisholm was a trader, not a cattleman, but the trail he blazed from his trading post in Wichita, Kansas to the Red River in Texas became crucial to cattle drivers. The trail was straight, with few river crossing and no large hills to navigate, and in some spots it was over 400 yards wide. This made the Chisholm Trail ideal for both trade wagons and driving cattle. Between 1867 and 1872, over one million head of cattle were herded from Texas to Kansas, where they were then loaded onto a train and shipped east.

Chisholm

The cattle trade in Dodge City was further fueled by an announcement that the AT&SF planned to build stockyards in the town. Railroad executives had been unsure about Dodge City's rather isolated location, but now it seemed ideal. On May 18, 1872, Captain D.G. Stockwell, a livestock agent for AT&SF, ordered that a 50 x 60 holding pen be built to house cattle. This structure was crucial in attracting cattle drives, because without a holding pen, it would be impossible to ship cattle out of Dodge City.

The Texas longhorns arrived via the cattle trails, and as the railroad moved west, so did the cattle trails. West of and just about parallel to the Chisholm Trail was the Great Western Trail, which started west of San Antonio in the town of Bandera, carved a path north past Abilene in West Texas, and kept going until it stopped in Dodge City. It was not as straight and easy to navigate as the Chisholm Trail, and it was drier and had small mountain ranges in Oklahoma Territory that offered a challenge to navigate, but it was still the most used of the cattle trails.

Cattle driving was a long and laborious process, so once the cowboys had directed their herd of cattle up the trail and into Dodge, most of them stayed put for at least a bit of time and looked for a chance to blow off some steam. Entertainment would quickly become available to accommodate them, as well as the wealthy cattle barons who passed through town. As both Texas longhorns and cattleman poured into Dodge City in the mid-1880s, it became a boomtown, similar to mining boomtowns of the era like Tombstone. However, the major difference between being a cattle town and a mining town was that Dodge City had a far more transient population. Thousands passed through, but very few stayed, and the locals were fine with that. When the AT&SF hosted one of its propaganda tours for 200 newspaper reporters from around the country to show the promise of Dodge City, few of the actual inhabitants in town were impressed. They had no interest in attracting settlers to the region, seemingly well aware of their destiny being "the great cattle mart of the West."

By the time Dodge City was really rolling, it was a unique kind of boomtown, or at least it seemed to one of the original inhabitants, Robert M. Wright, who wrote a history of Dodge City in 1913. In *Dodge City: The Cowboy Capital*, Wright colorfully described the atmosphere:

> "I have been to several mining camps where rich strikes had been made, but I never saw any town to equal Dodge. A good hunter would make a hundred dollars a day. Everyone had money to throw at the birds. There was no article less than a quarter--a drink was a quarter, a shave was a quarter, a paper of pins a quarter, and needles the same. In fact, that was the smallest change. Governor St. John was in Dodge once, when he was notified that a terrible cyclone had visited a little town close to the Kansas line, in Nebraska. In two hours I raised one thousand dollars, which he wired them. Our first calaboose in Dodge City was a well fifteen feet deep, into which the drunkards were let down and allowed to remain until they were sober. Sometimes there were several in it at once. It served the purpose well for a time.

> "Of course everyone has heard of wicked Dodge; but a great deal has been said and written about it that is not true. Its good side has never been told, and I cannot give it space here. Many reckless, bad men came to Dodge and many brave men. These had to be met by officers equally brave and reckless. As the old saying goes, 'You must fight the devil with fire.' The officers gave them the south side of the

railroad-track, but the north side must be kept respectable, and it was. There never was any such thing as shooting at plug hats. On the contrary, every stranger that came to Dodge City and behaved himself was treated with politeness; but woe be unto the man who came seeking a fight. He was soon accommodated in any way, shape, or form that he wished.

"Often have I seen chivalry extended to ladies on the streets, from these rough men, that would have done credit to the knights of old. When some man a little drunk, and perhaps unintentionally, would jostle a lady in a crowd, he was soon brought to his senses by being knocked down by one of his companions, who remarked, 'Never let me see you insult a lady again.' In fact, the chivalry of Dodge toward the fair sex and strangers was proverbial. Never in the history of Dodge was a stranger mistreated, but, on the contrary, the utmost courtesy was always and under all circumstances extended to him, and never was there a frontier town whose liberality exceeded that of Dodge. But, while women, children, and strangers were never, anywhere, treated with more courtesy and respect; while such things as shooting up plug hats and making strangers dance is all bosh and moonshine, and one attempting such would have been promptly called down; let me tell you one thing - none of Dodge's well-known residents would have been so rash as to dare to wear a plug hat through the streets, or put on any 'dog', such as wearing a swallow tailor evening dress, or any such thing…

Here congregated people from the east, people from the south, people from the north, and people from the west. People of all sorts, sizes, conditions, and nationalities; people of all color, good, bad, and indifferent, congregated here, because it was the big door to so vast a frontier. Some came to Dodge City out of curiosity; others strictly for business; the stock man came because it was a great cattle market...; the cowboy came because it was his duty as well as delight, and here he drew wages and spent them; the hunter came because it was the very heart of the greatest game country on earth; the freighter came because it was one of the greatest overland freight depots in the United States, and he hauled material and supplies for nearly four hundred miles, supplying three military posts, and all the frontier for that far south and west; last but not least, the gambler and the bad man came because of the wealth and excitement, for obscene birds will always gather around a carcass."

Chapter 2: Dodge City's Law Enforcement

Picture of the Long Branch Saloon in Dodge City

The term "lawless" is often used to describe frontier towns, and though that's often an exaggeration, there truly was no law enforcement or any type of government in Dodge City at all during its first year of existence. A railroad town like Dodge City was bound to be a magnet for all types of people of questionable characters, and Dodge City quickly earned its dangerous reputation, which should come as no surprise given the mix of young Texas cattle drivers, abundant alcohol, and no marshal or sheriff. On top of that, the worst of Dodge City's brutality in its early years came from the gamblers who were attracted to the town, not the cowboys.

As Dodge City was becoming established, the closest marshal was 75 miles away in Hays. Deputy U.S. Marshal Jack Bridges stayed in Dodge City, along with his wife and baby, in the fall of 1872, and the *Dodge City Times* praised Bridges in 1882 when he became Dodge City's marshal, saying of him, "He is a cool, brave and determined officer, and will make an excellent city marshal. Jack's friends speak highly of him and of his integrity and bravery. He has done some fine service for the government, and upon every occasion, has acquitted himself with honor. He is a pleasant man socially, and has courage for any occasion." However, since he was a federal marshal in 1872, he was there to keep track of federal offenses such as stealing horses or liquor violations, meaning he had no authority over the chaos that descended on Dodge City in its first year.

Bridges

It's no coincidence that Boot Hill, the iconic local cemetery, soon followed. In September 1872, the first recorded murder in Dodge City occurred when a black man named Tex, who was going by the nickname "Black Jack", was shot by a gambler. The incident occurred in a crowd, so nobody was really sure why Black Jack was killed or who even fired the shot. Years later, when he was far from Dodge City, a man named Denver bragged that he had shot Black Jack in the head just for the fun of it. Robert M. Wright, who wrote a history about Dodge City, wrote in a chapter aptly titled "Populating Boot Hill":

> "THE first man killed in Dodge City was a big, tall, black Negro by the name of Tex, and who, though a little fresh, was inoffensive. He was killed by a gambler named Denver…There was a crowd gathered, and some shots were fired over the heads of the crowds, when this gambler fired at Texas and he fell dead. No one knew who fired the shot and they all thought it was an accident, but years afterwards the gambler bragged about it. Some say it was one of the most unprovoked murders ever committed, and that Denver had not the slightest cause to kill, but did it out of pure cussedness, when no one was looking. Others say the men had an altercation of some kind, and Denver shot him for fear Tex would get the drop on him. Anyhow, no one knew who killed him, until Denver bragged about it, a long time afterwards, and a long way from Dodge City, and said he shot him in the top of the head just to see him kick.

The first big killing was down in Tom Sherman's dance hall, some time afterwards, between gamblers and soldiers from the fort, in which row, I think, three or four were killed and several wounded. One of the wounded crawled off into the weeds where he was found next day, and, strange to say, he got well, although he was shot all to pieces. There was not much said about this fight, I think because a soldier by the name of Hennessey was killed. He was a bad man and the bully of the company, and I expect they thought he was a good riddance."

Not long after Black Jack's murder, a railroad worker killed a man named Jack Reynolds. The violence continued through the fall and winter of 1872, and the death toll related to gun battles was already 15. The violence and gunfights associated with the Wild West are often a product of exaggeration and imagination, but this was not the case during the first few months of Dodge City's existence.

The murders and other deaths left the early townspeople with the chore of deciding on a site for a cemetery. The official Dodge City Cemetery was not built until 1878, and before then, the deceased were laid to rest on a lookout point with a view of the Arkansas River lowlands. With the high price of lumber making the building of coffins all but out of the question, bodies were simply wrapped in a blanket and buried fully clothed, including with their boots. This was the origin of the nickname Boot Hill, even though people would later associate the name with the notion that the cemetery was for people who died "with their boots on" in a gunfight. It was said that Dodge City "had a man for breakfast" every day to keep Boot Hill populated, but one woman was also buried there. Alice Chambers, a local "dance hall girl," died of natural causes on May 5, 1878 and was the last person to be buried on Boot Hill.

A plaque now commemorating Dodge City's Boot Hill reads:

"This hill was not a pleasant place during the 1870s. It was covered with buffalo grass, prickly pear and soapweed and was used as a burying ground for drifters, troublemakers and unknowns from 1872 until 1879. As early as 1873, newspapers were reporting that some people in Dodge City were "dying with their boots on" and were being buried where you are now standing. There were no ceremonies for the dead, no markers on the graves, and wolves often dug up the bodies soon after burial. By 1879, when the city council ordered that all bodies be removed from this site, about 34 persons had been interred on Boot Hill. In 1916 most of the hill was excavated to make room for a new city swimming pool."

A picture of Boot Hill taken in 1959 by Billy Hathorn

    The people of Dodge City grew increasingly alarmed at the violence, so by early 1873, they hired Billy Brooks to try and maintain some semblance of order. "Buffalo Bill" Brooks brought with him the reputation of a fearless gunfighter, and he had previously been the marshal of Newton, which like Dodge City was a tough cowtown. Brooks was not tall, but he was sturdy, with long hair that touched his shoulders, and his weapon of choice while on duty was a Winchester rifle. Legend had it that while in Newton, he chased three drunken cowboys out of town and kept on chasing them even after he had been shot three times. Brooks stayed on their tails for 10 miles before turning around to get medical attention for his bullet wounds.

Brooks

    According to the locals, Brooks was engaged in no less than 15 gunfights in Dodge City during his first few weeks on the job, and he successfully scared off would-be criminals in manners that some considered unethical. He also had a way of enforcing the law in violent ways against people that the townspeople didn't consider criminal or even bothersome, making them wonder why Brooks was so quick to use his gun on certain people. While this initially sounded just like the type of lawman that Dodge City needed, the town lost confidence in him when an outlaw named Kirk Jordan engaged Brooks in a gun battle on Front Street. At that time, the town was little more than a large timber box, as the sidewalks, benches, and buildings were all made of wood. Since fire was a constant concern, large barrels of water were placed at regular intervals along the street in case a fire broke out. Three men were sitting on one of the wooden benches when they saw Jordan ride up to Brooks, dismount his horse and raise a rifle right at Brooks, who dove for cover behind a water barrel. Jordan fired one shot, and a bullet hole turned the barrel into a water fountain. Thinking that he had killed Brooks, Jordan took off. Brooks was not dead, but he was also apparently not interested in chasing down his would-be killer either.

Instead, he went into a saloon and showed the patrons the bullet that had struck the barrel. As water ran into the street, Brooks ordered a drink, leaving the men to wonder why he was having a whiskey rather than going after Jordan.

Dodge City couldn't very well have their marshal hiding out when killers were on the loose. After hiding Brooks for the night, a group of men smuggled him over to the train station. By the following day, his career as the lawman of Dodge City was over. It was later said that Brooks got in a gunfight with Wyatt Earp's brother Morgan after Morgan was chosen marshal in Butte, Montana over him. According to that story, the fight ended with Brooks taking a bullet to the stomach and Morgan taking one in the shoulder. Brooks would later be lynched by a mob in July 1874

In need of law enforcement after the departure of Brooks, Dodge City tried a vigilance committee, which worked for a time, at least until the vigilance committee caused problems of its own. Dodge City inhabitant Robert Wright explained, "Our very best citizens promptly enrolled themselves, and, for a while, it fulfilled its mission to the letter and acted like a charm, and we were congratulating ourselves on our success. The committee only had to resort to extreme measures a few times, and gave the hard characters warning to leave town, which they promptly did. But what I was afraid would happen did happen. I had pleaded and argued against the organization for this reason, namely: hard, bad men kept creeping in and joining until they outnumbered the men who had joined it for the public good-until they greatly outnumbered the good members, and when they felt themselves in power, they proceeded to use that power to avenge their grievances and for their own selfish purposes, until it was a farce as well as an outrage on common decency."

In March 1873, saloon owner Tom Sherman was seen chasing a patron out of his establishment with a gun. Sherman, a member of the vigilance committee, shot the fleeing man and walked up to him as he lay writhing in pain in the dirt. Sherman said that he might as well put the poor man out of his misery and shot him point blank in the head.

However, a few months later, on June 3, 1873, Sherman and another member of the vigilance committee, Bill Hicks, picked the wrong man to mix it up with when they shot and killed William Taylor. Taylor was an aide to Colonel Richard Dodge, commander of Fort Dodge itself, and Dodge immediately sent a telegram to the governor, who granted permission to send troops to Dodge City to arrest the shooters. The incident resulted in the arrest of six members of the vigilance committee and the conviction of Bill Hicks, but it obviously did not solve the town's law enforcement problem.

Two days after the arrest of the vigilance committee members, Charlie Bassett was named the first sheriff of Ford County. The native of New Bedford, Massachusetts was a Civil War veteran who stayed in the West after he mustered out at Fort Sill, Oklahoma, but Bassett would not go down in western lore in the same manner as his undersheriff, William Barclay Masterson.

Known to all as Bat Masterson, the native of Quebec was 19 years old when he and his brother Ed were hired to help grade the mile-long stretch of road where the AT&SF track would cut an east-west path through Dodge City.

Ed and Bat, along with their brother Jim, had left their family farm near Wichita to try and make a go of it as buffalo hunters, but unfortunately, the subcontractor that hired Bat and Ed returned to the East Coast without paying the men for their work. Shortly after the railroad reached Colorado, someone in Dodge City mentioned to Bat that the man who owed him his pay would be passing through town the following day, and rumor was the man had at least $2,000 on him. Masterson, accompanied by a buffalo hunter named Josiah Wright Mooar and a six-shooter, went to the train depot to recover his money, earning the attention and admiration of many in the crowd that would not be forgotten.

Bat Masterson

Charlie Bassett and Bat Masterson were just two of many notable lawmen that tried to keep law and order in Dodge City during its 10-year run as cattle town. Wyatt Earp was a lawman in Dodge City at various times, and, in 1875, he was joined for a period of time by his younger brother Morgan. Bat was elected sheriff in November 1877, and his younger brother Jim was a deputy in 1878 before becoming a marshal in 1879. Ed, the oldest of the Masterson brothers, served as both deputy marshal and marshal of Dodge City.

On Christmas Eve 1875, the citizens of Dodge City made an effort to reform and clean up the town. They elected P.L. Beatty, a local saloon owner, as the acting mayor until an election could be held, and Dodge City also passed a series of town ordinances. Among the ordinances, which included laws against disturbing the peace and the use of profanity in public, was a law that banned concealed weapons for everyone except sworn lawmen. Upon arriving in Dodge City, weapons had to be checked with a law enforcement official, who would issue a token in exchange for the gun. The token could then be turned in to retrieve weapons on the way out of town.

Bat Masterson (standing) and Wyatt Earp in Dodge City, 1876

However, none of these ordinances or lawmen were ever really able to tame Dodge City, and trying to do so ended up costing Ed Masterson his life. On the evening of April 9, 1878, Ed and Deputy Nate Haywood went to the Lady Gay Saloon to confront a crowd of drunken cowboys from Kansas City who were causing a ruckus. The Lady Gay was located on the south side of the tracks. It had been established that the north side of the tracks were for more refined establishments, while those looking for a wilder time should go to the south side establishments. Ed, known to be very mild-mannered, approached a man named Jack Wagner and said that he would need to take his gun, since guns were not permitted in Dodge City. Wagner turned over his weapon without complaint, and Ed gave the gun to Wagner's boss, Alf Walker, asking him to check it with the bartender.

Ed and Haywood left the Lady Gay without incident, but as they stood outside the saloon, Wagner staggered out, and Ed saw the revolver was back in his possession, tucked under his coat. This time, Ed tried to take the gun himself, which started a scuffle between the two men as a crowd gathered. Meanwhile, Alf Walker pointed a gun at Haywood's face and pulled the trigger as Haywood reached for his gun belt. Walker's gun misfired and Haywood was spared, but Ed was not so lucky. Wagner fired a shot directly into Ed's abdomen, setting Ed's coat on fire as the bullet passed through his body from right to left. Mortally wounded, Ed drew his gun and shot Wagner in the abdomen before firing three shots at Walker as well, putting one bullet into his chest and two into his right arm. Ed managed to walk 200 yards to Hoover's Saloon before collapsing at the feet of the bartender, George Hinkle. Ed died within the hour, and Wagner died the next day and was buried at Boot Hill. No charges were filed against Walker since Wagner confessed on his deathbed that he shot Ed Masterson, and Walker eventually recovered and left Dodge City, never to be seen there again. Bat arrested the companions of Walker and Wagner, but with no proof that they were involved in his brother's killing, they were released without charges being filed.

Chapter 3: Dodge City Entertainment

The Long Branch Saloon

By 1875, the number of men in Dodge City outnumbered women by a margin of six to one, so naturally, the vast majority of entertainment in Dodge City was geared toward male patrons. This meant Dodge City had the typical mix of saloons, dance halls, billiards rooms, theaters, and brothels, and the owners of the establishments changed so fast that it was nearly impossible to keep up with who was responsible for what operation.

During the day, Dodge City was often a sleepy town, and a lot of barkeeps had so little to do that it was not unusual to see them sitting in front of the saloon watching the day go by. Cowboys were either working or sobering up enough to safely get on their horses and ride. But Dodge City came alive at night, with music wafting through the streets as cowboys sampled the local whiskey, faro tables, and ladies of the evening. The most famous of Dodge City's entertainment establishments was the Long Branch Saloon, which owed its beginning to a wager in 1873 between cowboys and a group of soldiers from Fort Dodge. The soldiers and the cowboys were playing baseball, and, likely fueled by a beer or two, the soldiers agreed to provide the materials to build a brand new saloon in town if they lost the game. The soldiers lost, and they kept their word, so it was not long before the Long Branch Saloon appeared on Front Street.

The original owners and proprietors of the Long Branch were Sheriff Charlie Basset and A.J.

Peacock. Peacock also already owned the Billiard Saloon, which opened in 1872. The Long Branch featured a long bar along one wall, a billiards table in the front, a gambling room, and for the customers who had one too many whiskeys, a room for "sleeping it off."

The interior of the Long Branch Saloon

In 1878, Chalk Beeson and William Harris bought the saloon, and the Long Branch became known as a proper establishment for the refined tastes of the cattleman who came to town. Beeson was a businessman, but he was also a musician who liked to play his violin for the Long Branch patrons, and in 1879, Beeson's Dodge City Cowboy Band began to entertain the saloon's customers. Dressed in traditional cowboy garb, including flannel shirts, leather chaps, boots with spurs, and holsters with pearl-handled revolvers, the five-piece orchestra was under the leadership of Beeson in its early days. Beeson went so far with the cowboy theme that instead of a baton, he conducted the orchestra with a revolver. The Cowboy Band played at festivals and cattleman conventions all over the West, and they were even invited to play at President Benjamin Harrison's inauguration on March 4, 1889.

Chalk Beeson

Beeson's Cowboy Band

The Cowboy Band was one of many traveling entertainment troupes who were actually professional musicians from around the country, but they looked every bit the part of Kansas cowboys. Some locals did not like the way they played up the cowboy image of Dodge City, especially because they were trying to ensure Dodge City transitioned away from its wild reputation, but the crowds they played to loved it.

Prizefighting

Prizefighting was illegal in Ford County, but that did not mean that it did not happen. Bat Masterson, who would spend the last two decades of his life as a New York City sportswriter, saw his first fight in Dodge City. Considering that he was a lawman at the time, he was legally obligated to arrest the principle parties involved in the fight, but he solved that problem by taking off his badge, and it's also quite possible that he asked for a "fee" to allow the fight to take place.

On June 16, 1877, the *Dodge City Times* reported on a prize fight between the favorite, Nelson Whitman, and Red Hanley, known as "The Red Bird from the South". At stake was the championship of Dodge City, but few people knew when and where the bout was going to take place. The fight got underway at 4:39 a.m. in front of the Saratoga Saloon, an unusual start time chosen to keep out of sight of the local law enforcement, who by that time had concluded their evening of rounding up cowboys who had one too many shots of whiskey.

The newspaper's account of the fight shed some light on why the sport was banned:

"On last Tuesday morning the champion prize fight of Dodge City was indulged in by Messrs. Nelson Whitman and the noted Red Hanley, familiarly known as 'the Red Bird from the South.' An indefinite rumor had been circulated in sporting circles that a fight was to take place, but the time and place was known only to a select few. The sport took place in front of the Saratoga saloon at the silent hour of 4:39 a. m., when the city police were' retiring after the dance hall revelry had subsided and the belles who are in there were off duty. Promptly at the appointed time, the two candidates for championship were at the joint. Colonel Norton acted as rounder-up and whipper-in for both fighters while Bobby Gill ably performed the arduous task of healing and handling and sponging off. Norton called time and the ball opened with some fine hits from the shoulder. Whitman was the favorite in the pools but Red made a brilliant effort to win the champion belt.

"During the forty-second round Red Hanley implored Norton to take Nelson off for a little while till he could have time to put his right eye back where it belonged, set his jawbone and have the ragged edge trimmed off his ears where they had been chewed the worst. This was against the rules of the ring so Norton declined, encouraging him to bear it as well as he could and squeal when he got enough. About the sixty-fifth round Red squealed unmistakably and Whitman was declared winner. The only injury sustained by the loser in this fight were two ears chewed off, one eye busted and the other disabled, right cheek bone caved in, bridge of the nose broken, seven teeth knocked out, one jawbone mashed, one side of the tongue bit off, and several other unimportant fractures and bruises. Red retires from the ring in disgust."[2]

Boxing was brutal enough, but the townspeople witnessed even more barbaric games, including a contest that took place a few weeks before the championship prizefight. On May 12, 1877, the *Dodge City Times* reported:

"We, yesterday, witnessed an exhibition of the American national game of lap-jacket, in front of Shulz' harness shop. The game is played by two colored men, who each toe a mark and whip each other with bull whips. In the contest yesterday, Henry Rogers, called Eph, for short, contended with another…for the championship and fifty cents prize money. They took heavy new whips, from the harness shop, and poured in the strokes pretty lively. Blood flowed and dust flew and the crowd cheered until Policeman Joe Mason came along and suspended the cheerful exercise. In Africa, where this pleasant pastime is indulged in to perfection, the contestants strip to the skin, and frequently cut each other's flesh open to the bone."

The Fourth of July Bullfight

---

[2] Robert M. Wright, *Dodge City: Cowboy Capital,* http://www.skyways.org/orgs/fordco/wright/13.html

In the summer of 1884, Dodge City was already changing. Settlers were coming into the region and farming land, families were replacing the gamblers and prostitutes, and the town was slowly losing its grip on its title as the "Queen of Cowtowns." Many people welcomed the change, but some of the original residents did not want to see things change. However, even if it did have to change, some thought that Dodge City could go out with a bang instead of whimper. That bang was the first bullfight on American soil.

Staging a bullfight required an arena, and former mayor Alonzo Webster was put in charge of the planning and fundraising efforts. Within one day of presenting the plan to an enthusiastic town council, Webster had raised $10,000, and the fight was scheduled for July 4, 1884, giving the town just six weeks to prepare. Dodge City began to fill with tourists, cowboys, and reporters from as far away as New York to see the event, but the town was ready in time.

Reaction to the event was mixed. Some locals were anxious to show off Dodge City, but many felt the whole thing was distasteful, and local clergy urged a boycott. It was made clear that the fight would be "to the death," which caught the attention of the American Society for the Prevention of Cruelty to Animals. The ASPCA's founder, Henry Bergh, sent letters and telegrams to Governor George Glick, asking him to put a stop to the "atrocities", but Glick would not hear of it and even said he would have attended if he did not already have plans.

The bullfight became part of a larger multi-day festival. Independence Day was on a Friday, and the festival kicked off on Wednesday with a horse race and a roping contest. Thursday featured another horse race and a shooting competition, but everyone was looking forward to Friday. By noon on the Fourth, Front Street was lined with horses. As many as 700 cowboys came to town, and hundreds more spectators filed out of the railroad cars to head for the brand new arena. Over 4,000 people, more than three times the population of Dodge City itself, jammed into the grandstands to watch Gregorio Gallardo lead his bullfighters in a battle against a dozen Texas bulls.

Most of the bulls disappointed the paying crowd and did not put up much of a fight. It was only when a large red bull was led into the arena that the fans got the action that most had come to see. They wanted to see bloodshed, and they got it when the bull fell to Gallardo's 150-year old sword, although not before the bull pinned the matador up against a gate and injured his ribs. There was a second fight on Friday which did not result in bloodshed but thrilled the crowd nonetheless.

Despite the naysayers, the town got what it wanted. Merchants got customers, the fans were entertained, and Dodge City was able to hang on to its image, even if its status as a great Western cowtown was rapidly coming to an end that summer.

Dora Hand

Just as the chaos of Dodge City seemed to be settling down, along came Dora Hand and a 23 year-old cowboy named James "Spike" Kenedy. Hand's real name was Fannie Keenan. Possibly a former opera singer, she was known as the "Queen of the Fairy Belles," which was a euphemism for dance hall girl. Before arriving in Dodge City, Hand had performed in St. Louis, Memphis, and New Orleans. Kenedy was the son of a wealthy cattleman, and plenty of townspeople later claimed Kenedy acted like he was entitled; in his biography on Bat Masterson, Robert DeArment noted that Kenedy "liked whiskey, whooping and whoring, and as heir to the Kenedy fortune, he considered himself immune to arrest by cow-town marshals." After Kenedy got into a gunfight in Dodge City in 1872, his father used his influence to get his rash son out of trouble, but Spike constantly mixed it up with authorities. In the summer of 1878, Deputy Marshall Wyatt Earp arrested him for carrying a pistol.

Hand's first gig in Dodge City was as a singer at the Comique (pronounced com-ee-cue by the cowboys), a theater owned by Ben Springer. The Comique took its name from the Theatre Comique in New York, but it made no attempt to present itself as respectable as its New York City namesake. Admission to the Comique was free, but the steady supply of alcohol kept the cowboys and gamblers reaching for their money, and the entertainment at the Comique was still first rate. Well-known comedian and dance Eddie Foy was one of the artists who entertained the crowds at the Comique, in addition to Dora Hand, who was well liked around town and known to not hesitate to help others. Whether it was tending to the sick or helping young cowboys get back home after losing all their cash at faro, Hand was willing to help. In fact, her generosity rubbed off on others and motivated them to pay more attention to the people in town who were in need. Hand's stage persona seemed to be just that. She was a performer by night but a respectable, even demure woman by day. It is also likely that Hand was a prostitute, but few if any women of the frontier chose that profession willingly. It was usually simply a matter of survival.

Hand became a featured performer at the Alhambra Saloon and Gambling House, and if Dodge City had a rising star, she was it. She had caught the attention of the saloon's co-owner, Mayor James "Dog" Kelley, who was often seen around town with Hand. Sometime in July or August 1878, Kelley got into an argument with Spike Kenedy. Some say it was over the amount of attention he was giving to Hand during one of her shows, but either way, Kelley physically removed Kenedy from his bar one night. Kenedy paid a fine for disturbing the peace and left town. Masterson biographer DeArment explained, "Kenedy nursed a bitter hatred for the Dodge City law officers, but he lacked the backbone to take up a personal fight with any of them. Instead, he expressed his grievances to Mayor Kelley one night in Kelley's own establishment, the Alhambra. Kelley informed him that the marshals were acting under his orders and that young Kenedy had better behave while in Dodge or prepare himself for worse treatment. Kenedy then flew into a rage and leaped at the mayor. Kelley gave the younger man a thorough beating and dumped him in the street. Kenedy was furious. Mouthing dark threats against the life of the mayor, he mounted up and rode out of town. No one in Dodge expected to see him again."

However, Kenedy wanted revenge for the humiliation and planned an attack on Kelley's house behind the Great Western Hotel a few months later. What he did not know was that Kelley was letting Hand and another singer from the Comique, Fannie Garretson, stay at his place while he was out of town getting medical treatment. On October 4, 1878, Kennedy went to Kelley's house and fired two shots at his door before speeding away toward Fort Dodge. Wyatt Earp and Jim Masterson went to investigate and discovered that one of the shots went through the wall that divided the two bedrooms. Garretson slept in one room and was unharmed, but Hand was in the second room when a bullet hit her in the chest as she slept, killing her almost instantly. On October 8, the *Ford County Globe* reported, "The first shot, after passing through the front door, struck the floor, passed through the carpet and facing of the partition and lodged in the next room. The second shot also passed through the door, but was apparently more elevated, striking the first bed, passing over Miss Garretson, who occupied the bed, through two quilts, through the plastered partition and, after passing through the bed clothing of the second bed, struck [Hand] in the right side, under the arm, killing her instantly."

There were no solid witnesses to the shooting, but when authorities headed to the scene, they were told Kenedy had done the shooting. Figuring Kenedy would flee back to his father's place, Masterson, Earp, and some other lawmen rode out of town in an attempt to catch up with Kenedy. When they did, Kenedy tried to bolt, only to have Masterson shoot him in the shoulder as Earp downed his horse. As he lay bleeding, Kenedy asked them if he had killed Kelley, only to hear that he had actually killed Dora Hand. Kenedy looked to Masterson and said, "You ought to have made a better shot than you did." To that, Masterson told him, "I did the best I could."

Kenedy was hauled back to Dodge City to stand trial, but he was ultimately acquitted, likely due to his father's deep pockets. The *Ford County Globe* reported on October 29, "Kennedy, the man who was arrested for the murder of Fannie Keenan, was examined last week before Judge Cook and acquitted. His trial took place in the sheriff's office, which was too small to admit spectators. We do not know what the evidence was or upon what grounds he was acquitted." Speculation abounded that Kenedy's father had paid off important people in Dodge City, including Bat Masterson himself.

As for Hand, her funeral was well attended, drawing hundreds of people who wanted to pay their final respects to the performer and Dodge City resident. Describing the scene, one witness claimed, ""Every store, saloon and gambling house in Dodge closed during the funeral, and 400 men with their sombreros on their saddle horses rode behind the spring wagon that carried Dora Hand up Boot Hill."

Chapter 4: The Dodge City War

Given that Dodge City was basically a saloon and a few tents when it was established, it should be no surprise that liquor was at the center of Dodge City politics. Many of the buffalo hunters that helped create it stayed in town to open up saloons or work in them as bartenders, and a few became lawmen as well as proprietors of saloons. By 1877, Dodge City's population was just under 1,000, but those residents had several drinking establishments from which to choose, including 16 saloons and plenty of brothels and dance halls as well.

For obvious financial reasons, a contingent of local politicians, lawmen, and merchants were intent on keeping the whiskey flowing. The cowboys that came up from Texas on cattle drives had money to spend, and the businessmen of Dodge City wanted to see to it that the cowboys were quickly separated from that money. The group was informally called the Dodge City Gang, and their leader was Dog Kelley, Dodge City's mayor from 1877-1881. Kelley's business interests were tied to the Alhambra Saloon, the site of the events that led to the death of Dora Hand in 1884.

Even with some of the West's most iconic names as lawmen, Dodge City remained a rough and tumble town, and the Dodge City Town Council tried to address that by passing ordinances in 1878 that outlawed gambling and prostitution, two of the town's biggest draws. Anyone who was caught engaging in these activities was fined but not subjected to jail time, making the ordinances not much of a deterrent to the gambling halls and brothels that remained open. In fact, the money that the fines generated brought in additional funds to city coffers that helped pay the lawmen's salaries. For the Dodge City Gang, it was business as usual.

However, not everyone in Dodge City was happy with the reputation of their town. They were give the name The Reformers, and by 1879, they built a following of citizens who opposed the business dealings of The Gang. The Reformers saw no way to clean up Dodge City if the very men charged with maintaining law and order were profiting from gambling, prostitution, and alcohol. Thus, it would require removing The Gang from power.

The Dodge City Gang and the Reformers were the participants in what came to be known as the Dodge City War. There were no shots fired in this war, but it was a battle for the control of Dodge City itself.

In the fall of 1879, one of the Gang was defeated in a tightly contest race for Ford County sheriff when George T. Hinkle beat Bat Masterson. While it was true that Hinkle also owned a saloon, he was not a member of The Gang, and the defeat sent Masterson out of Dodge City, albeit temporarily. Meanwhile, the Reformers rejoiced.

Then, in the elections of April 1881, Dog Kelley lost his seat as mayor to Alonzo Webster, and all pro-Gang town council members were also swept out of office. Webster, a Union cavalry veteran who had also made his way to Kansas in the Civil War, was a local merchant who had had owned a dry good store since 1872, as well as two saloons, but he was not part of the Dodge City Gang. Webster made that clear on April 17 when he posted a notice: "To all whom it may concern: All thieves, thugs, confidence men, and persons without visible means of support, will take notice that the ordinance enacted for their special benefit will be rigorously enforced on and after tomorrow." To make sure that the ordinance was enforced, Jim Masterson was replaced as city marshal by Fred Singer, a bartender in one of Webster's saloons.

Jim Masterson

Earlier in 1881, Jim Masterson and A.J. Peacock went in on the Lady Gay Dance Hall and Saloon. Al Updegraff, Peacock's brother-in-law, was hired to be a bartender. There was always some tension between Jim and Updegraff, and Jim eventually wanted him fired, but with Updegraff being part of Peacock's family, Jim was not going to win that argument. For reasons that are not clear, Updegraff swore a complaint for Jim's arrest, which prompted someone in Dodge City to send a telegram to Bat that read, "COME AT ONCE. UPDEGRAFF AND PEACOCK ARE GOING TO KILL JIM." At this time, Bat was in Tombstone, Arizona, helping run faro tables for Wyatt Earp, but having already had one of his brothers killed in Dodge City, he returned immediately in case trouble broke out.

On April 16, 1881, Bat arrived in Dodge City and immediately went to see Updegraff and Peacock. As Bat rode the train into town, he saw Peacock and Updegraff walking, so he jumped off the train as it was still moving and said to them, "Hold up there a minute, you two. I want to talk to you." Upon seeing Masterson, Peacock and Updegraff ran toward the city jail as Masterson stood near the railroad tracks. Exactly who fired first is not known, but bullets started flying. Other men jumped into the fray, and Dodge City quickly had a full-scale gun battle on

Front Street. When all was said and done, Bat was arrested and Updegraff had a bullet wound in his lung that was serious but not life threatening. It was only after the gunfight that Bat learned the two men had not hurt his brother Jim at all.

Given all the commotion, it was impossible to know with certainty who had shot Updegraff, so Masterson was only given an $8 fine. After paying the fine, Bat left Dodge City again, and this time Jim went with him after Peacock bought out his share of their saloon. Tom Nixon, assistant marshal, then bought the Lady Gay, the town's remaining dance hall.

Dodge City suddenly did not look much different than it did when the Gang ran it. Politicians and lawmen were still running saloons and dance halls, and now the only difference was that the money collected for fines was going to pay the salaries of Alonzo Webster's lawmen instead of Dog Kelley's.

The Long Branch Saloon became a prominent fixture in news again with the arrival of a renowned gunfighter named Luke Short in 1882. Short became part owner of the saloon, along with his friend, W.H. Harris, and Short was also friends with Wyatt Earp and Bat Masterson. He had recently been in Tombstone, plying his trade as a gambler, but he was no thug. Short was good at his trade and liked to spend his money on clothes. He was not a large man, but he was feisty and fearless.

Luke Short

Harris was also a gambler, as well as a cattleman and the founder of the first bank in town. He ran for mayor against Lawrence Deger in 1883, and the two men were squarely on different sides. Harris was associated with the Gang, and Deger was in with Mayor Webster, who wanted Deger as his replacement. Deger already had his own reasons for not liking the Masterson brothers too; Bat Masterson beat him in the election for sheriff in November 1877 and Ed Masterson had replaced him as city marshal.

The mayoral election was no contest, due largely to mudslinging from the Deger campaign, and rumor had it that railroad men may have stuffed the ballot box to make sure Deger won. The AT&SF had tried to reform the town's lawless ways and even threatened to remove its station, and this caught people's attention. The railroad had enough influence to get saloons closed on Sundays, music barred from dance halls, and a restriction on gambling, although only for a short period of time. When Bat was marshal, he had been unable to protect the railroad and its property as drunken cowboys shot out the train headlights and fired on the railroad crews, so conductors carried weapons to ensure they could collect fares. However, the problem with the railroad's threats was that Dodge City brought in too much money for the AT&SF to follow through and move the station. In 1884, 800,000 head of cattle and 3,000 passengers used the railroad to go east out of Dodge City.

On April 28, 1883 three prostitutes from the Long Branch were arrested under the city's ordinance against "vice and immorality," even though no other working girls at other saloons had been arrested. Short considered this a personal attack on him and his business, and he was right. Webster and Deger did not like the company that Short kept, and they also did not much care for the fact that they couldn't compete with the Long Branch. The majority of patrons at Dodge City establishments were Texans who favored Short and his Texas roots.

That same night, Short went to the city jail with revolver on each hip. New policeman had recently been brought in, and Short encountered one of them. Louis C. Hartman, who was also the city clerk, was on the sidewalk outside of the jail. Gunfire broke out, but it was not clear who fired first. Whoever started it, Hartman fell to the ground but was not hurt. He then ran for cover and fell off the sidewalk. Short thought he killed Hartman and ran to the Long Branch and barred the door. After he was told that he did not kill Hartman, Short surrendered, was charged with assault, and released on a $2,000 bond.

A few days later, Short and five other gamblers were arrested and ushered to the train station. They were given their pick: go east or go west but get out of Dodge City. Short got on an eastbound train to Kansas City, where he sent a telegram to Bat in Denver. Bat told him to go to Topeka and ask for a meeting with George Glick, the governor of Kansas. Glick was known to support alcohol sales and could be sympathetic to the fact that Short had literally been railroaded out of town. Meanwhile, the May 9, 1883 edition of *The Kansas City Evening Star* reported that the lawlessness of Dodge City had reached the point that the governor may have to put the town under martial law, as it was currently under control of "vigilantes."

The governor sent a telegram to Sheriff George Hinkle to ask what was happening in his town, and, in particular, what had happened with Short. Hinkle replied that Short had been kicked out of Dodge City because he did not follow town ordinances, which Governor Glick thought nothing short of ludicrous. Glick replied that if Mayor Webster preferred to bypass the legal system and encourage mobs to run citizens out of town, he had no business being the mayor.

Soon after that, Short went back to Kansas City, where he was joined by Bat Masterson, Charlie Bassett, Wyatt Earp, and a quirky dentist turned gambler named Doc Holliday. Hinkle had heard that Short and his associates would be returning to Dodge City, so he ordered a posse to monitor all inbound trains. Earp did return to Dodge City on May 31 with four of his associates, but he was met at the train station not by Hinkle's posse but also by "Prairie Dog" Dave Morrow, the town constable and a friend of Bat Masterson. Earp asked Morrow if he would deputize him and his friends, which would allow them to legally carry guns in Dodge City. Morrow, agreeing that Short was treated badly, deputized the five men, and they became known as the Dodge City Peace Commission.

When the governor refused Webster's request to send a militia, it became apparent to Webster that the best course of action was probably to compromise, and the two sides ultimately reached an agreement on gambling and prostitution. Gambling could occur in areas separate from bars and dance halls, and prostitutes could continue to discreetly ply their trade. Short was allowed to return to Dodge City, but he and Harris sold the Long Branch in November 1883 and Short moved on to Fort Worth, Texas. Earp and Bat Masterson left town too, but not before posing for a photo with their fellow Peace Commission members.

The "Dodge City Peace Commission". From left to right, standing: W.H. Harris, Luke Short, Bat Masterson, W.F. Petillon. Seated: Charlie Bassett, Wyatt Earp, Frank McLain

and Neal Brown.

Peace and compromise had won in Dodge City. It was the sign of things to come.

Chapter 5: A Cattle Town Dies and a Legend is Born

The end of Dodge City's time as a cattle town came quickly and with little fanfare. Men who had been clamoring to get in on the cattle business just three or four years earlier were no longer interested, and many who had stock in cattle companies sold their shares. More importantly, Texas longhorns developed a tick that caused splenic fever, and the spread of the disease resulted in quarantines in Kansas and Nebraska. By 1885, Texas cattle were banned east of the Kansas-Colorado border, ensuring there would be no more cattle drives passing through Dodge City.

That was not the only disaster to strike Dodge City in 1885. In January, an article in the *Kansas City Cowboy* pointed out what a good deal fire insurance companies were getting by selling their product in Dodge City. The town had never experienced a devastating fire, and the article's author theorized that the fact that the local businesses were rarely closed probably had something to do with the fact that all fires were quickly extinguished. Ironically, the very next day, a fire started in a grocery store basement and made its way up and down Front Street. Despite the efforts of hundreds of people to fight the fire, seven businesses were destroyed, including the *Kansas City Cowboy* printing office. Then, on November 27, 16 businesses were destroyed in another fire as the locals spread salt on roofs and threw buckets of water at burning buildings. The fire destroyed Dodge City's business district. As if that was not enough, another city block was destroyed by fire on December 7, destroying Dodge City mainstays like the Long Branch Saloon, Delmonico's Restaurant, and Hoover's Liquor Store.

Front Street in 1885

In 1886, Dodge City's first fire station opened, and P.L. Beatty was the first fire chief. Wyatt

Earp, Ed Masterson, and Chalk Beeson were just a few of the volunteer firefighters. Still, the destruction of the buildings from Dodge City's early years signaled a transition to something new, and the Long Branch and the other original establishments along Front Street were not rebuilt. By 1887, they were replaced by brick buildings, and with that, Front Street lost a bit of its frontier character for something a bit more mainstream. As the West was settled and Dodge City's rough character was tempered, the town's population steadily climbed from just under 2,000 to its current peak of 27,000.

Dodge City's heyday as a frontier town lasted only 10 years, but Hollywood has kept the image of Dodge City as a Wild West town alive long after that era ended. Over time, separating Dodge City's reality from its legend has become difficult, and many historians point to Stuart Lake's biography of Wyatt Earp, *Wyatt Earp: Frontier Marshal*, as the true beginning of the Dodge City legend. Published in 1931, the book was wildly popular, but modern historians agree that it is more of a work of fiction than a true account of Earp's life. In addition to glorifying Earp, Stuart glorified Dodge City, even though Earp had far more of an impact in Arizona than in Kansas.

By the 1930s, after Wyatt Earp and Bat Masterson had died, American media was in the midst of a love affair with the iconic West that would last until the 1960s. Films featured the mythical Dodge City as their setting, starting with "Dodge City" in 1939. It starred Errol Flynn as sheriff Wade Hatton, the man charged with taming lawless Dodge. However, it was Marshal Matt Dillon that cemented the image of the Dodge City lawman in the minds of just about anyone who watched television between 1955 and 1975. For 20 years, James Arness played Marshal Dillon on "Gunsmoke," one of the longest running television shows in history. Set in Dodge City, "Gunsmoke" also featured Amanda Blake playing the role of Miss Kitty, the local madam and proprietor of the Long Branch Saloon, with Ken Curtis playing Marshal Dillon's scraggly deputy Festus and Milburn Stone playing the wise Doc Adams.

"Gunsmoke," which was already a popular radio program, came to television just as interest in the Wild West was hitting its peak. Four days after the debut of "Gunsmoke," "The Life and Legend of Wyatt Earp," starring Hugh O'Brian as Marshal Earp, hit the airwaves on ABC. "Wyatt Earp" was on the air for six seasons, and most of them set in Dodge City. In 1958, "Bat Masterson" debuted and ran for three seasons, with Gene Barry playing the part of Masterson. Many other westerns followed, including "Bonanza," "Have Gun – Will Travel," "The Rifleman," and "Rawhide." Many of these shows have lived on in syndication, earning them new generations of fans.

Much has been made of America's reverence for the West. Some argue that it is a longing for simpler times, but a study of the West and the people who lived on the frontier clearly demonstrates that just surviving was a struggle. Others point to America's love of heroes, and Hollywood's western heroes are easy to spot, even if the actual lawmen of the West lived complex lives and straddled both sides of the law. Part of the appeal of Dodge City is due simply to the fact that it provided a backdrop for colorful stories to play out.

For many people, Dodge City is a living monument to history, even if it's an exaggerated and embellished version of history, but even as many residents in Dodge City tried so hard to erase the town's reputation in the 1870s, modern day Dodge City does its best to keep the frontier reputation alive. The town capitalizes on its iconic history for the sake of tourism with the Gunfighters Wax Museum, the Boot Hill Museum, and the Trail of Fame walking tour through its historic downtown. It's safe to say that, just like the people of the Old West themselves, the famous places of the West will continue to be icons with just the right mix of truth and fiction to teach and fascinate new generations about one of the most unique eras of American history.

Bibliography

Agnew, Jeremy. *Entertainment in the Old West.* Jefferson, NC: McFarland & Company. 2011

"Cowtowns." Kansas State Historical Society. http://www.kshs.org/kansapedia/cowtowns/15598

DeArment, Robert K. *Bat Masterson: The Man and the Legend.* Norman, OK: University of Oklahoma Press. 1989.

Schillingberg, William B. *Dodge City: The Early Years, 1872-1886.* Norman, OK: University of Oklahoma Press. 2009.

Snell, Joseph W. and Don W. Wilson. "The Birth of the Atchison, Topeka, and Santa Fe." *Kansas Historical Quarterly, Vol. 34, No. 3.* 1968. Kansas State Historical Society. http://www.kshs.org/p/kansas-historical-quart...atchison-topeka-and-santa-fe-railroad-2/13188

Vestal, Stanley. *Dodge City: Queen of Cowtowns.* Lincoln, NE: University of Nebraska Press. 1998.

Wright, Robert M. *Dodge City: Cowboy Capital.* State Library of Kansas. http://www.skyways.org/orgs/fordco/wright/13.html

Tombstone

Chapter 1: The Birth of Tombstone

In 1877, Ed Schieffelin was working for the U.S. government as an Indian scout in Arizona. After leaving the Grand Canyon area, Schieffelin moved south and was stationed at Fort Huachuca, not far from the Mexican border. As he was known to do, Schieffelin went out on his own to search for "rocks", hoping to find his own riches. Other soldiers in the camp told him that the only stone he would find out in the rugged hills was his tombstone. When he found silver, the soon-to-be millionaire named his first mine "The Tombstone."

An 1880 portrait of Ed Schieffelin

Part of the interior of Schieffelin's mine

Within a month of Ed Schieffelin's discovery of silver in the rugged hills of southeastern Arizona in 1877, a small town sprang up to provide food and lodging for the prospectors. But this small town would not share the name Tombstone with Schieffelin's mine. The tiny village was called Watervale, due to the nearby well.

It made sense at the time that a town would spring up near the closest water source, but Watervale may have lost a future claim to fame due to that location. Watervale was somewhat inconvenient for the miners who started streaming into the region looking to strike it rich because it was three miles away from the silver mines. In an era before automobiles rode down paved roads, asking miners to travel an extra three miles over a dusty, rocky road after a day of hard labor was asking a lot.

The second town to develop near the Tombstone and Lucky Cuss mines was also not Tombstone. The unnamed site at West Site Mine was 100 yards southeast of what locals now call Old Firehouse Number 1. It did well at first, attracting a post office, a saloon, and a few eating establishments. And ironically, one of the earliest proprietors of the town was Ike Clanton, who would become notorious for his role in the famous Gunfight at the O.K. Corral a few years later.

Ike Clanton in 1881

Ike Clanton may have managed to stay out of trouble if he had the opportunity to remain the owner and operator of the Star Restaurant on that site, but the West Site Mine location had just 10 acres, leaving it no room for growth. To make matters worse, in February 1879 a ferocious windstorm whipped through town and leveled everything in sight. Thus, during the following month, local businessmen decided to survey land on what eventually became Tombstone. 320 acres of land were divided into zones, and streets were laid out. Streets running north and south were numbered, and streets running east and west were named for prominent citizens, including Arizona's territorial governor, the famous explorer John C. Fremont. After their evening meal, some miners pitched in and helped clear roads from the mines to the camps until there were four roads leading into Tombstone. The town did not have its own water source, but hauling in water on wagons from Watervale solved that problem.

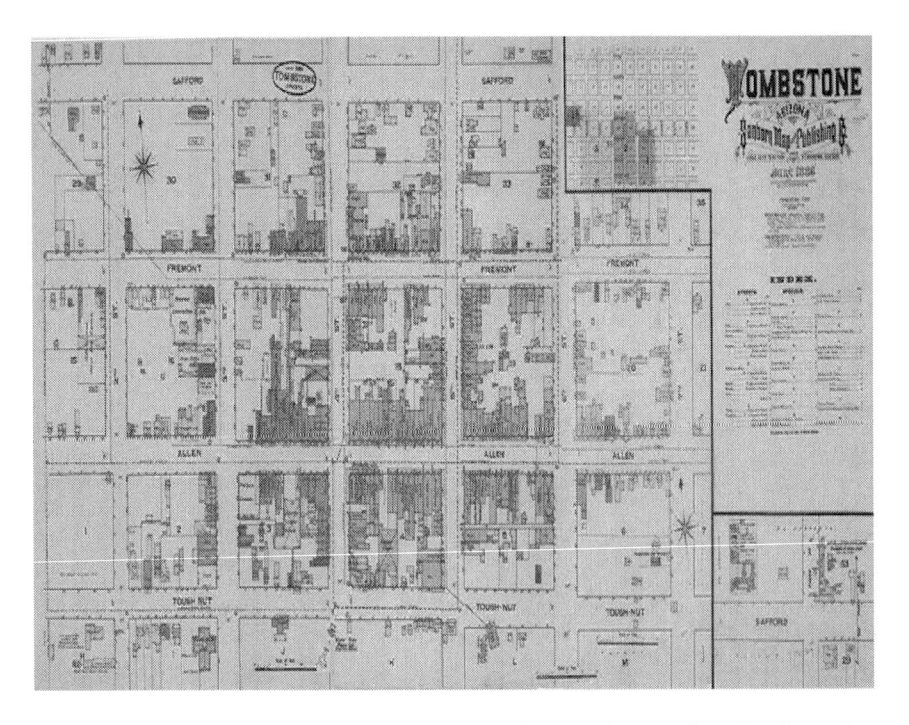

A map layout of Tombstone in 1888 shows the main roads Fremont St., Allen St., and Tough Nut St.

There were initially three primary mines: Lucky Cuss, Contention, and Toughnut. By the time Tombstone was in the process of being built, Toughnut had already had so much work done on it that silver ore was being piled on the ground. The next step that remained was to haul the silver ore to the stamp mill for crushing.

There were numerous tunnels and shafts dug into Toughnut and Lucky Cuss, some as long as 75 feet. Two shafts had been dug out of Contention, both over 100 feet long, and workers had carved a 250-foot tunnel. It was in these shafts and tunnels that miners would spend their days and nights.

Entrance to the Toughnut Mine

A mule train at one of the Tombstone mines

The walls of the mines were made of limestone and hard porphyry that had to be either drilled by hand or blasted by dynamite. Ore was lifted out of some of the mineshafts to the main shaft by using a windlass, a method of lifting heavy objects that dates back to the Middle Ages. The windlass had to be cranked by hand, which made for slow going for the men operating the apparatus. Once ore made it to the main shaft, it was dumped into a large bucket called a kibble and lifted out using a 20-horsepower engine. From there, the ore was put into wheelbarrows, and teams of mules hauled ore to mills.

Schieffelin's Tombstone Milling and Mine Company hired miners to work in two shifts of 10 hours each, meaning that miners were working long days and there was very little time during the day when mining was not in progress. For light below ground, miners used stearin candles. In an era when it was not unusual to make one or two dollars per day, miners in Tombstone were paid well. They made $4 a day, and bricklayers, carpenters, and mechanics could make anywhere between $5-7 per day. It was not long before businesses arrived in Tombstone, designed to separate workers from their hard-earned wages.

Chapter 2: People and Businesses Come to Tombstone

The first structures to go up in Tombstone were simply tents on plots of land. Wooden and adobe buildings only came later; after all, the first residents of Tombstone had little reason to think the town would be around very long. Back then, it was not unusual for a town to spring up near a mine one day and be gone the next, depending on the fate of the mine or discoveries nearby. Tents were less of an investment in time and money, and given the fact that Tombstone was located on the frontier, there were few building supplies available in the town's early days. Hauling in lumber from the Huachuca or Dragoon Mountains was not cheap either; it cost anywhere between 50 and 65 dollars per 1,000 square feet. With little time to waste, tents filled in until permanent structures could be built.

The difficulties involved in actually constructing the town of Tombstone were made evident by the fact that Tombstone's first hotel was a tent. The Mohave Hotel was later named Brown's after owner Charley Brown, one of Tombstone's founding residents. Brown was a native of Ohio, and when he moved west he got involved in steam boating and mining. Brown also spent some time as a shopkeeper in a store that he owned. He opened his first hotel, the Cosmopolitan, in Portland, Oregon, and his first hotel in Tombstone opened on April 14, 1879. The Mohave, located at Fourth Street and Allen, brought in about 20 visitors a day, which induced Brown to quickly expand. He opened up a Chinese restaurant too, as did Sam Sing about two months later. Brown would eventually own one of the biggest hotels in the town, as well as the building that housed the Hafford Saloon, a favorite hangout of Wyatt and Virgil Earp.

Interior of the Hafford Saloon

It's no surprise that hotels were among the first businesses to take hold in Tombstone, since miners making their way to the camp needed somewhere to sleep and eat. There was plenty of business to go around for hotel operators. After the Mohave opened, the affordable San Jose Lodging House opened at Fifth and Fremont. The San Jose was owned by one of Tombstone's original female entrepreneurs, Samantha Fallon. Fallon was a rare breed in the Tombstone of 1879, since the vast majority of Tombstone's original residents were men.

Jessie Brown owned one of the most elegant hotels in Tombstone, the Grand Hotel. The sheer opulence of the structure stood in stark contrast to the dirt, dust, and occasional stench of the mining town. Brown made sure that the three-story hotel was filled with the finest furnishings, which she had shipped in from San Francisco, and one of the first things that guests noticed when they entered the hotel was the wide staircase, covered in expensive carpet with a banister made of black walnut. The second floor featured a parlor that dazzled guests with silk-covered furniture and rare oil paintings. Each of the 16 rooms had wallpaper, beds with spring mattresses, matching furniture and carpet, and toilet stands for holding perfumes and other toiletries.

The most impressive feature of the Grand Hotel may have been that all rooms faced out to the street, so they each had a window. The ability to open a window for ventilation was an important feature in the early days of Tombstone. For the Grand's dining room, Brown hired a chef who specialized in French cuisine, but she also made sure that her menus were printed in English so that customers could actually read them. Brown started a trend with her English menus, and other French restaurants in town soon followed her lead. Three elegant chandeliers hung from the dining room ceiling, and the walnut dining tables were set with china and cut glass. The kitchen, which had a 12-foot stove and both hot and cold running water, was capable of making enough food to serve up to 500 people a day.

The cleverly named local paper, the *Tombstone Epitaph*, described the Grand Hotel in September 1880:

> "Through the courtesy of Mr. H.V. Sturm an Epitaph reporter yesterday paid a visit to and made a brief inspection of the new hotel christened the grand which will be formally open for dinner this evening at five o'clock. The general size and character of the structure have been mentioned so often during the course of construction that further mention would be superfluous and we will confine ourselves to a description of the interior appointments of it. Passing into the building by the front entrance the first thing that strikes the eye is a wide and handsome staircase covered by an elegant carpet and supporting a heavy black walnut banister. Thence upstairs to the main hall, and turning to the right we are ushered into a perfect little bijou of costly furniture and elegant carpeting known as the bridal chamber. This room occupies half of the main front and is connected with the parlor by folding doors through which the reporter passed, and entering the parlor was more than astonished by the luxurious appointments. A heavy brussels carpet of the most elegant style and finish graces the floor, the walls are adorned with rare and costly oil paintings; the furniture is of walnut cushioned with the most expensive silk and rep, and nothing lacks, save the piano which will be placed in the position shortly. On down through the main corridor peeping now and then into the bedrooms, sixteen in number, each of them fitted with walnut furniture and carpeted to match: spring mattresses that would tempt even a sybarite, toilet stands and fixtures of the most approved pattern, the walls papered, and to crown all, each room having windows. All are outside rooms thus obviating the many comforts in close and ill-ventilated apartments. Returning we pass down the broad staircase and turning to the left are in the office and reading room. Here we met Mr. R.J. Pryke, the polite and affable clerk, so well known to Yosemite tourists in California. The office fixtures are as is common in first class hotels and fully in keeping with the general character of the house. The dining room adjoining next invites inspection. Here we find the same evidence of good taste in selection and arrangement that is so marked a feature of the whole interior. Three elegant chandeliers are pendant from the handsome centerpieces, walnut tables, extension and plain, covered with cut glass, china, silver castors and the latest style of cutlery are among the many attractions of this branch of the cuisine.
>
> Thence into the kitchen where we find the same evidence before mentioned; an elegant Montagin range 12 feet in length, with patent heater, hot and cold faucets, in fact all the appliances necessary to feed five hundred persons at a few hours notice

are present. The bar occupies the east half of the main front and is in keeping with the general furnishings. Want of space prevents more than this cursory glance at the Grand and its appliances for the comfort and convenience of guests. A Grand (no pun intended) invitation ball will take place this evening."

Unfortunately, the Grand Hotel was destroyed by a fire in 1882, and Big Nose Kate's Saloon was built in its place. That saloon was named after the famous girlfriend of Doc Holliday, an association made all the more ironic by the fact that Ike Clanton and two of the McLaury brothers stayed at the Grand Hotel the night before facing Holliday in the Gunfight at the O.K. Corral.

Big Nose Kate's Saloon today

Big Nose Kate

    Across the street from the Grand Hotel was Tombstone's other landmark hotel, the Cosmopolitan. It also started as a tent, but even when it was still only a tent, it was the first hotel in Tombstone to offer beds. The Cosmopolitan was so popular that it did not take long for the owner, Gus Bilicke, to earn enough money to expand. By 1880, the Cosmopolitan added a second story. As guests milled through the hotel lobby, they were treated to sounds of Bilicke playing his Steinway piano. When visitors and investors arrived in Tombstone in its heyday, the twin structures of the Grand and the Cosmopolitan exuded money and opportunity.

Picture of the Cosmopolitan

Once it became clear that Tombstone was going to be around at least awhile, markets soon followed. A well-stocked market from Watervale relocated to a brick building on Fremont Street, and three other markets opened in Tombstone in the fall of 1879, two of which featured fresh produce and dairy products from California. When flour, eggs, and butter eventually made their way to Tombstone, fresh baked goods began to be featured on menus as well. But it was no easy feat getting those goods to Tombstone at the time; they were delivered to Tucson by rail and then hauled to Tombstone by wagon, a 13-hour trip in the late 19th century.

As 1879 drew to a close, Tombstone was still a mining town, no matter how much it was growing. The people that lived and worked there primarily worked in the mining industry, and the businesses that opened were there to serve them. Boarding houses charged $20 a month for rent and another $8 for food and other essentials. Most restaurants charged about 50 cents for dinner and less than that for breakfast and lunch. For those miners who opted to save money by camping out and cooking for themselves, a pound of bacon cost 12 cents, coffee and sugar went for 20 cents a pound, and potatoes could be had for two cents a pound.

When people spoke of Tombstone in 1879, they were still calling it a "camp". That would change in 1880.

Chapter 3: Tombstone Becomes a Town

Growth

Tombstone began to take on a more permanent look during the winter of 1879-1880. Tents gave way to adobe structures, Tombstone elected its first mayor at the end of 1879. The first newspaper, the *Weekly Nugget*, printed its debut edition on October 2, 1879, and in 1880 the first members of Tombstone's city council were appointed. When the national census was taken in 1880, Tombstone had 2,100 residents. By the time a special census was taken in Arizona in 1882 to accounting for the new counties that had sprung up in the past two years, Tombstone reported 5,300 residents, second only to Tucson. At its peak, as many as 15,000 people crowded Tombstone's dusty streets.

Stagecoaches were bringing in new arrivals every day, but newcomers to the area had to learn to adjust to the southeastern Arizona climate. The sun was bright and hot in the summers, and though winters were milder than back east, it still got cold enough to require a fire. With no trees in the area other than mesquite, miners quickly discovered that burning the roots was almost as good as burning coal.

Most of the people coming to Tombstone still hoped to strike it rich as miners, but those who were not silver miners made other business opportunities for themselves by providing the typical business services. A number of notable dignitaries passed through Tombstone, including Joseph Goldwater, an ancestor of Senator Barry Goldwater, and George Hearst, who made his money in mining unlike his son, publishing magnate William Randolph Hearst. It was the wealthy patrons that truly pushed Tombstone toward its reputation as the most cosmopolitan town on the western frontier. Investors with deep pockets and their wives expected a lifestyle of elegance and privilege, even in a boomtown like Tombstone.

Joseph Goldwater

 As Tombstone grew, so did its sophistication. Before long, it was not just the Grand Hotel that offered fine dining. Tombstone came to have restaurants that rivaled those found in San Francisco, both in cuisine and style. French cuisine was all the rage in the Victorian era, but there were other options too, including Chinese, German, Italian, Irish, and Italian restaurants. Of course, this was still Tombstone, and dust had a way of getting in every nook and cranny of the town. If there was water to spare, the town took to watering down the streets and sidewalks to keep the dust at bay. Summer months brought stifling heat and flies, but neither of these things was a deterrent for those wanting to go out for a nice meal. More than the customers, it was the cooks and kitchen staff of restaurants who suffered during the hot weather. With no air conditioning in the kitchens and none of the modern conveniences, simply making a stock or a dressing by hand was hard work.

 Tombstone is now considered one of the Old West's iconic towns, but it was very much under the influence of the East in its early days. The first three mayors and the first three marshals of Tombstone were Easterners, and even by 1880 Tombstone was too cosmopolitan for Ed Schieffelin and his brother Al. that year, they sold their interests in the Tombstone Mining and Mill Company just as the company was peaking. Ed was not one for "city" life, and he was willing to settle for $600,000 even though the value of the holdings of the Schieffelin brothers was probably closer to $2 million.

 With Ed and Al heading off to Nevada to do more prospecting, the Tombstone mining company was left in the hands of wealthy businessmen from the East coast. The company owned nine different mines by this point, and just as importantly, it owned the water rights for 20 miles of land that ran all the way from Tombstone to the Mexican border. In addition to the prosperous mines, they owned mills that converted the silver ore to bars. In just a few months, spanning June 1879 to March 1880, one of those mills produced silver bars worth over $316,000. The company eventually produced over $100,000 in silver per month.

Transportation

The high volume of silver being hauled out of Tombstone's mines led most to believe that the next logical step in the town's progression was a railroad depot. The local businessmen began calling for one starting in the spring of 1880 after the Southern Pacific Railroad carved a route through the town of Benson, 28 miles north of Tombstone. To get from Tombstone to Benson took over 5 hours, and while that was less than half the time it took to get to the train station in Tucson, it was still not a quick trip. Businessmen and residents alike agreed that it was not simply a matter of moving people in and out of town. In order for business and commerce to grow, there needed to be a freight terminal for the goods and silver moving in and out of town. Mills were located along the San Pedro River, and people in the mining industry thought it was essential to have a railroad system for transporting the silver ore to the mills.

Despite the urging of the business community, the railroad was slow to arrive in Tombstone, leaving the town to rely on horse-drawn wagons, stagecoaches, and similar methods of transportation during its early years. This transportation arrangement made Tombstone a target for cowboys seeking to rob wagons and steal goods flowing in and out of the town, and one of those robberies would ultimately lay the groundwork for the Gunfight at the O.K. Corral. The railroad got closer in 1882 after 88 miles of track for the New Mexico & Arizona line was laid from Benson to Nogales, just north of the Mexico border. The line went through Fairbank, just nine miles from Tombstone, and the N.M.&A. was part of the larger Atchison Topeka & Santa Fe line, which had plans to compete with the Southern Pacific. The intent was for the N.M.& A. to be a major foothold in southern Arizona and to include a branch line to Tombstone.

However, the project never got off the ground, and the Santa Fe dropped its plan to build a presence in southern Arizona. Tombstone's glory years were relatively short, and railroad companies were hesitant to invest much time and money expanding into the region. It was not long before the price of silver declined and Tombstone's mines flooded, neither of which helped Tombstone's prospects of getting a railroad depot. It would require the boom of copper mining in Bisbee to get the railroad to Tombstone; in July 1901, the El Paso & Southwestern Railroad began laying track to connect the mines of Arizona with the smelters in El Paso, Texas and Douglas, Arizona. Tombstone is about 20 miles south of Bisbee and Douglas is about 20 miles east of Bisbee.

Of course, Tombstone was long past its prime at the beginning of the 20th century, but Tombstone was experiencing a bit of a mining resurgence, thanks mostly to E.B. Gage. Gage was an entrepreneur in the mining industry who understood the successes and challenges of Tombstone's earliest mining ventures. He formed the Tombstone Consolidated Mines Company in June 1901, which merged several of the smaller independent mining companies in the region. When he approached the El Paso & Southwestern Railroad about building a line to Tombstone, the company agreed. Without it, Gage's plan to consolidate the mines would never have worked. Gage's company ultimately built nearly 10,000 feet of the track, using Mexican and Native American laborers.

After laying track in Fairbank on March 9, the first tracks were finally laid in Tombstone on March 24, 1903. On April 12, approximately 2,000 people crowded the streets of Tombstone to celebrate the railroad's arrival. One of the local newspapers, *The Tombstone Prospector*, published a 56-page commemorative edition in recognition of the long-awaited event.

The El Paso & Southwestern eventually merged into the Southern Pacific and operated a line into Tombstone until 1960, one year after the last mine in town closed.

Law and Order

The image of Tombstone as a town where upstanding sheriffs battled gangs of rogue bandits is largely a myth. There was certainly a criminal element, due to the amount of money coming in and out of Tombstone and its relatively close location to the Mexican border. In general, lawlessness was a fact of life in the West because towns often sprung up before law enforcement arrived. Tombstone was no different, but as the population of Tombstone grew, the workers of the town selected men to enforce the law.

On December 9, 1879, the Pima County Board of Supervisors incorporated Tombstone as a village. With that, Tombstone was permitted to appoint a town marshal, pass town ordinances, and establish a justice of the peace and court. Among the first ordinances were bans on sleeping on the streets, making indecent gestures, racing horses faster than six miles an hour in city limits, and using profanity in public. Occasionally, the town also tried to enforce some limits on guns, and even though most of the townspeople didn't like it, most of them abided by the expectation that they check their guns with the bartender when they entered a saloon.

Historic Tombstone Courthouse

In 1881, the town passed an ordinance banning the wearing of concealed weapons. The ordinance was aimed primarily at gamblers, who were more likely to sit down at a gaming table with a small gun tucked in a pocket. That summer, the *Daily Nugget* published an editorial that said, "The revolutionary fathers, who put this into the bill of rights, did not go around with little pistols concealed in their hip pockets; they carried their rifles and muskets over their shoulders like men…If it is the proud right of a freeman to bear arms, why should he conceal them?"

Cattle rustling cowboys caused some problems with Mexicans by going south of the border to steal cattle and horses and then sell them to ranchers around Tombstone. When Mexican law enforcement cracked down on the smuggling and the Mexican government set up forts to protect the border, cowboys started to steal from Arizona ranchers and sell the cattle and horses to the Mexicans instead. The head of the most well known "gang" of cowboys was Newman "Old Man" Clanton. The term gang was used loosely in the Old West, since there was no formal gang of cowboys, but Old Man Clanton and his sons, Ike, Phineas, and Billy, ended up in Arizona after fleeing the law in Texas and California. Another notorious outlaw, William "Curly Bill" Brocius, was associated with the Clanton family, and Frank and Tom McLaury also had a ranch nearby the Clanton property. Billy Clanton and the McLaury brothers would meet their demise in the famous gunfight at the O.K. Corral. Curly Bill would also be involved in one of Tombstone's most notorious events.

Old Man Clanton

The businessmen that made their way to Tombstone wanted stability, law, and order. Chaos and lawlessness did little attract investors, nor did it help Arizona's efforts to become a state. However, law and order on the western frontier was not easy to achieve. When Wyatt, Virgil, and Morgan Earp came to Tombstone, they aligned with the Republican businessmen from the East Coast and attempted to preserve law and order in the name of Tombstone's economic stability. This would ultimately pit the Earps and their friend Doc Holliday against cowboys and cattle ranchers like the Clantons and McLaurys. On top of that, many of the cowboys and ranchers were former Confederate sympathizers who believed in a small government, placing them squarely at odds with the Republican business establishment.

Newman Clanton died in August 1881, just a few months before one of his sons was killed in the Gunfight at the O.K. Corral. Before his death, the Clanton gang had raided a band of Mexican smugglers that was traveling through the Skeleton Canyon of the Peloncillo Mountains. The Clantons made off with silver, cattle, and mescal totaling about $4,000. Likely in retaliation, Newman Clanton and a group of his men were attacked in Guadalupe Canyon a few days later as they were driving cattle to Tombstone from New Mexico. The attackers are believed have been troops from a nearby Mexican fort. Old Man Clanton was killed in the attack.

More killings followed that, and the tension along the Arizona-Mexico border now got the attention of the federal government. President Chester Arthur told Congress in December 1881 that the problems at the border were complicating relations with Mexico. Arthur wanted to use federal troops in the region, but Congress refused to authorize it. Within Tombstone, problems with the cowboys would create a rift between two contenders for the new position of sheriff of Cochise County: Johnny Behan and Wyatt Earp. That rivalry would add another layer to the subsequent Gunfight at the O.K. Corral.

Nevertheless, the majority of men in Tombstone were law-abiding citizens. Miners worked 60 hours a week, leaving them little time to get into bar fights or locked up in jail. The men in Tombstone could certainly be rowdy – many were young men far from home who could get into trouble after a few drinks – but that did not necessarily lead to violence. Robbery and gunplay were the exception, not the norm.

Churches

Churches became part of Tombstone from the time the first miners arrived. Like everything else, the first churches were tents, and seats were simply boards placed across boxes. A Methodist Episcopal church had its first services in a wooden shack with a torn canvas roof, and that shack also served as a theater. Preachers giving sermons on Sundays might have to battle with the noise from a nearby dance hall, but churches were one of the few places of refuge for townspeople who were typically not well received in the community. Even the ladies of the evening who would typically be seen in saloons looking for customers at night could also be found attending Sunday services during the day.

In August 1880, the walls of a permanent Episcopalian church went up, but rain slowed the construction of the adobe exterior. The editor of the *Epitaph,* John Clum, wrote an editorial encouraging the local businessmen to raise money for the funds needed to finish the church. Clum pointed out that there was likely no town as big as Tombstone that also lacked a church. In 1882, construction also began on a permanent Catholic church.

Chapter 4: Entertainment

Mining was very difficult work, which meant that almost all of the miners were young men. The work was also as monotonous as it was tiring. If a prospector was working on his own claim, his days were spent in the dusty arroyos or in the canyons looking for silver. If a man worked for a mining company, as most did, he spent 10 hours a day below ground digging and drilling. When the day was done, it was back to his tent or some type of shack for a dinner of pork and beans if he could not afford a boarding house or did not want to pay for one. With no sanitation system, the mining camps were not only dirty but also unhealthy. Dysentery, malaria, fever, and diarrhea were common, made all the more dangerous by the lack of quality medical care.

Diseases were that much easier to catch thanks to the presence of rats, which raided miners' shacks at night. Cats were valuable to miners because they tracked down the rats, but they were scarce in Tombstone's early days because they could easily be stolen. Dogs were useful too, primarily because they served as alarm systems and warned those on the edge of town if an

Apache raiding party was on its way. But rumor had it that the Apaches were afraid of dogs, so dogs were stolen from miners by other miners too. Eventually, Tombstone was so overrun with dogs that the town had to pass an ordinance requiring dogs to be licensed. Failure to abide by the ordinance could result in a dog being impounded and euthanized.

It was not an easy life, and it definitely led to the need for some entertainment to serve as a diversion. This led to the growth of businesses designed to allow the miners and other residents to blow off steam. Saloons, gambling houses, and bordellos were open 24 hours a day, seven days a week. Like Las Vegas today, Tombstone never closed.

Bordellos

Tombstone was a man's town during its heyday, which made the presence of at least one kind of woman necessary. When miners were streaming into Tombstone, business was good for the local madams. Their pleasantly decorated bordellos and ladies clad in evening gowns were welcome in a town that was often choking with dirt and dust. The ladies of the evening also provided welcome companionship to lonely men who were often far from home. In Tombstone, prostitution was a legal form of business and was not hidden. In fact, prostitution was expected, and there were plenty of townspeople who took issue with gambling but had no complaints about what happened in bordellos. Some women even freelanced out of their own homes with no outside interference.

The youngest and the prettiest women found regular work in the bordellos. Older or less attractive women were relegated to finding customers in saloons or renting a shack, called a crib, for three dollars a day. Reasons for engaging in prostitution varied. Some women simply did it for the money because it paid better than being a seamstress, one of the few occupations available to women in Tombstone at the time. Some of the women worked in the bordellos part-time and were entertainers at other times. For a great number of women, prostitution was the difference between being able to eat or not, so it was strictly a means of survival.

One reason so many people accepted prostitution was that the money generated by it could be used for more noble pursuits. Bordellos were required to have a business license, which provided funding for the school system for years. The buildings were also used as facilities to care for sick people if an illness was spreading through the town, since the women that worked there could be used to tend to those that needed care.

Theaters

Several theaters were up and running in Tombstone by the summer of 1880. Allen Street had the Danner and Owens Hall, which featured a roomy auditorium, elegant chandeliers, theater boxes, and velvet curtains. The Sixth Street Opera House, which came to be called the Free and Easy, was open that summer too, as was Ritchie's Hall and the Turn-Verein Hall.

Fittingly, the biggest and most famous theater in town was Schieffelin Hall, considered the finest theater between El Paso and San Francisco. Funded by Ed Schieffelin himself, it was two stories tall with a 24-foot ceiling and a 40-foot wide stage. The hall, which seated 700 patrons, hosted a wide variety of operas, musicals, plays, and lectures.

Schieffelin Hall

As fine as the Schieffelin Hall was, the miners were not as interested in the theater as they were in the entertainment at the Bird Cage Theater. It was owned by William J. Hutchinson, a former stage performer who bought the lot that the Bird Cage stood on for $600 when Tombstone was just getting started. The Bird Cage opened on December 23, 1881 and was an instant hit. For 50 cents, people filed in and watched dancing girls perform skits, work as barmaids, and make money on the side as prostitutes, all of which attracted cattle rustlers, cowboys, miners, and smugglers alike. The skits were far from refined, but that was the point; the bawdy shows were just what the clientele wanted as they stood with drinks in hand, watching the performances on a stage that was about 15 feet tall, 15 feet wide, and 5 feet above the ground. Gas jets near the front of the stage provided stage lighting.

The Bird Cage Theater

When the shows ended around 2:00 a.m., the chairs and tables were pushed aside to create a dance floor. One of the most popular performers was Pearl Ardine, who newspapers said could dance a jig, reach down to grab money tossed her way, and stow it away in her stocking, all without missing a step. Mrs. De Granville had a strong woman act and was billed as the "woman with the iron jaw" for her ability to pick up heavy objects with her teeth. A comedienne named Nola Forrest performed at the Bird Cage in 1883. When she left town, it was discovered that the bookkeeper, J.P Wells, had stolen more than $800 to keep Forrest supplied with jewels. On one occasion, a performance of the stage version of "Uncle Tom's Cabin" prompted a drunken cowboy to shoot a dog in the play. The furious crowd beat him to a pulp before he could be arrested, and the following day the remorseful man tearfully offered up his horse and his money to pay for the loss.

The name of the Bird Cage came from the 14 "bird cages" that were placed high on the walls overlooking the first floor. A stairway led up to private boxes where ladies of the evening could provide one-on-one entertainment for customers, and red curtains were drawn around the individual cages for privacy. The basement of the theater had a gambling hall, another bar, and private rooms for prostitutes to ply their trade.

The popularity of the theaters and the stage productions led to a new town ordinance in April 1881. Theaters had to pay a $5 tax for every day that a stage production was held in the facility, which amounted to a hefty revenue maker for the town. But that didn't deter the theaters, and theatrical troupes streamed into Tombstone in the early 1880s. Nellie Boyd's "Dramatic Company" played for three weeks at Ritchie's Hall in November 1880, all to standing room only crowds. Her visit was so popular that she brought her production to Tombstone many times over the next three years. The vaudeville actor and comedian Eddie Foy played at the Bird Cage, remarking that it looked like a coffin. Robert McWade, Jr., who would go on to act in silent movies, performed at the Six Street Opera House, and the stove and bar had to be removed to add an additional 150 seats.

A countless number of magicians, ventriloquists, lecturers, and other types of performers also graced the stages of Tombstone during its heyday. Minstrel shows were just as popular in Tombstone as they were in other parts of the country. Local residents also enjoyed taking their turn on the Tombstone stages. Mayor John Clum was one of the locals who caught the acting bug, and Ed Schieffelin wrote an original song called "Tombstone Camp" that was featured in a benefit. Mayor Clum was at that benefit too, and after reciting a poem he joined a quartet to sing a song. Tombstone also had its own glee club, which made its debut at the Oriental Saloon, another favorite hangout of Wyatt and Virgil Earp.

John Clum

Local actors also helped raise money for the town in the summer of 1881. A fire had swept through Tombstone, and the young town did not even have a fire alarm to alert the citizens. The Tombstone Dramatic Relief Association put on a play at Schieffelin Hall and sold tickets for $1. The troupe raised $400, which was used to buy the town's first fire alarm.

Gambling

There were several options for entertainment other than the arts, and gambling was at the top of the list. Compared to other frontier towns, Tombstone's gambling halls and saloon gaming tables were considered high class. Many miners chose to go to their favorite saloon when their workday was done, and they frequently stayed there all night. Saloons made up for the lack of organized entertainment with cheaper beer and liquor, and almost all of them had some type of gaming table. Popular choices were faro, roulette, and poker, and most tables were filled with gamblers at every hour of the day since the saloons did not close. It was not unusual for a miner to stay at a saloon until the sun came up and go to work directly from the poker table.

Gambling was a vice, and with that vice came corruption. The fairness of the games largely depended on the proprietor, and even the players to some degree. There was a code of ethics that all of the gambling halls were expected to follow, but it was a loose set of rules. After all, the whole point of the gaming tables from the owner's perspective was to make money for the saloon, and they would do what they could to slant the odds in their favor while still observing the code of ethics. It was also not unheard of for a more seasoned card player to take advantage of a less experienced player by using a deck of marked cards.

Some of the most famous images of the Wild West include barroom brawls and card players sitting at their seat with their guns in their holsters. There is some truth to the mythical image of a gun-toting card player. Amateur players were usually not armed, but professional card players typically had more than one gun on them. A Colt .45 revolver might be sitting on a table or in the player's lap, while a smaller caliber gun, sometimes called a "pepper-box," was hidden in a pocket or a boot. These smaller weapons were easier to fire, and the fact that they were easily hidden was also a plus. Miners just in town for a relaxing game of poker understood that the professionals were armed, so miners generally did not argue with them and risk getting shot.

Another popular form of gambling was cock fighting. This was long before most people cared about treating animals humanely, and it was long before cock fighting was outlawed. In fact, it was not outlawed in Arizona until 1998. The roosters used in the fights in Tombstone were generally from Mexico, most often from nearby Sonora, but sometimes they came from as far south as Chihuahua.

Cock fights in Tombstone were often for high stakes matches, and hundreds of dollars could be bet on just one match. The overhead was low since all that was needed was a vacant lot, which was easy to find in Tombstone. A rope served as a ring, and a local resident would be trusted with the duties of the emcee. Once the handlers set the roosters in the ring, the birds fought to the death as the crowd cheered. When one match was complete, the next pair of roosters was brought into the ring and the excitement started all over again.

Horseracing was also a common form of gambling. Horses had a special meaning in the days of the Western frontier. As important as the car is today, horses served the same purpose in the late 19th century. Those who liked to brag about their horses were able to settle disputes about who had a faster horse by staging a race, which also gave the locals something else to bet on. Native Americans also competed in the horse races, with some making the trip from Tucson to not only race horses but also buy and sell them too. Unfortunately for some of the horse traders, they often lost their cash as quickly as they made it when bootleggers preyed on them and sold them whiskey.

Sports

In the days before hunting and fishing licenses, those activities were available to the people of Tombstone whenever they wanted. There was no official season. The biggest issue was risking a confrontation with a Native American who did not want a hunter or fisherman encroaching on his territory. The San Pedro River was a common spot for fishing, and a hunter could find quail, deer, and even bear in the Huachuca and Dragoon Mountains.

Major League Baseball had not been formed yet, but baseball was still popular in the frontier days. Around 1882, George Rice started a baseball team called the San Pedro Boys. The Tombstone Baseball Association squad came after that and played for nearly 40 years. One of Tombstone's finest athletes was Endicott Peabody, who was a 25 year old baseball player, boxer and preacher. The local newspaper made note of his ball-playing abilities some time after his arrival from Massachusetts in 1882, saying, "We've got a parson who doesn't flirt with the girls, who doesn't drink behind the door, and when it comes to baseball, he's a daisy."

Peabody, known as Cotty to friends and acquaintances, was not just there to play baseball. He had accepted a request from Grafton Abbot, also from Massachusetts, to go down to Tombstone to serve as a sorely needed Episcopal minister. Abbott said to Peabody that Tombstone was "the rottenest place you ever saw." Not surprisingly, as more baseball teams formed, they too became an outlet for the town's gamblers. The problem was finding an umpire who was trusted enough to not have his own side bet on the game, which might influence how he judged a close play.

Peabody

Peabody solved that problem and agreed to umpire the games, but he did so under one condition; he would only be an umpire after the players and the fans went to church. This led to an array of miners, businessmen, and even some ladies of the evening crowding into Reverend Peabody's services. No doubt this pleased Peabody, who initially had a hard time getting anyone but the social elite of Tombstone to come to church. Eventually, Peabody was the referee for all of the outdoor games. He was trusted by all and did not play favorites. He was also known to put on a pair of boxing gloves, and he earned the everlasting respect of the town when he defeated the larger Methodist minister, Joseph "Mac" McIntyre.

Of course, Peabody was not there just to play ball or box; he was there to help build a church. When he first arrived, it had been six months since the town's only church had burned down, so he held services in a room at the Miner's Exchange Building. The town had raised over $1,000 to go toward building a church, but the money was kept in a bank that also burned in the fire. This meant fundraising was his first order of business. He was not above strolling into a saloon and hitting the miners up for a donation, and on one occasion he was startled to see one of Tombstone's wealthier citizens, the general manager of a mine, drop $150 into his donation bucket. Peabody was even more surprised when all of the other players at the table did the same. The grateful Peabody told the men that they would never regret it.

Unfortunately for Tombstone, Peabody's time in town was brief. Peabody returned to the East on July 17, 1882, and many of the locals were sad to see him leave their community. He had helped raise almost $5,000 for St. Paul's Episcopal Church, complete with stained glass windows and gothic arches. It was built at 3rd Street and Safford, where it still stands today. St. Paul's is the oldest Protestant church in the state of Arizona and is on the National Register of Historic Places. It is also thought to be the West's oldest Episcopal church.

St. Paul's Episcopal Church in Tombstone

As for Peabody, two years after he left Tombstone he founded the prestigious Groton School in Groton, Massachusetts. Among the students at Groton was Franklin Delano Roosevelt. Reverend Peabody officiated Franklin and Eleanor's wedding in 1905.

Chapter 5: Tombstone's Chinese Heritage

As the Southern Pacific Railroad made its way through southeastern Arizona, hundreds of Chinese immigrants arrived in Tombstone and surrounding areas to find work. The majority of immigrants came from the overpopulated and poverty-stricken Guangdong province, and many of the earliest Chinese immigrants were sent to the U.S. through an association called the Chinese Six Companies, which is still in operation today.

Chinese workers had their passage to the U.S. paid by the association and, in turn, they had to pay the association back with wages they earned. That took years because Chinese workers were usually paid less than other workers. The association also took care of workers when they were sick and served as a bank for the immigrants, who often did not trust the U.S. banking system. Given the number of bank robberies and stagecoach hold ups, they had valid concerns.

However, after the railroad construction jobs ended, the Chinese workers were left unemployed. Any jobs that remained went to white workers, so the Chinese spread out across southern Arizona looking for jobs wherever they could find them. The mining boom led many to Tombstone. Initially, the residents of Tombstone were wary of the immigrants, who obviously looked quite different. Few were taller than 5 feet tall, and according to Chinese government requirements; the men wore their hair in a pigtail. As was also the case with railroad workers, Chinese immigrants avoided drinking water unless it was boiled and made into tea, because unsanitary conditions often contaminated the water supplies. And while many Tombstone miners sopped up beans or gravy with bread, the Chinese used chopsticks.

The Chinese were not welcome in most saloons and gambling halls. In fact, they were not even counted in the Arizona census, nor were their marriages recorded in county records. They were, however, welcomed as workers. Chinese immigrants were willing to do hard labor for less pay, and as railroad executives discovered, they were typically very efficient workers. Still, the immigrants tried to avoid confrontation with Tombstone residents by setting up their own Chinatown neighborhood. The Chinese residents often made their way through town using private tunnels, and at one point there were about 500 Chinese residents in Tombstone's Chinatown, called Hoptown by the whites.

Not surprisingly, Chinatown had its own forms of entertainment. Card games were as popular there as they were in the white section of Tombstone, but the games were different. Mah Jong was also popular, and opium took the place of whiskey for the Chinese, who also had festive celebrations for Chinese New Year. The Chinese living in Chinatown also had access to their own doctors, grocers, acupuncturists, and temples, which also served as meeting halls.

One of the most well known Chinese residents of Tombstone was called China Mary by the locals, keeping with the tradition of calling just about all Chinese women by the American name Mary. She was such a fixture in Tombstone that she even earned a spot in an episode of the 1960s television series "Wyatt Earp", played by actress Anna May Wong. A rotund woman often colorfully dressed in brocaded silk, China Mary was well respected throughout Tombstone. She was married to a man named Ah Lum, but they presumably divorced because he wound up marrying a Mexican woman named Antonia Gomez.

China Mary was in the labor business, operating what amounted to a temporary employment agency. A white man or woman would go to China Mary to ask about hiring a Chinese worker, and they paid China Mary, not the worker. Business was good because she guaranteed the work. If the job was not done well, she saw to it that the job was done again or the work was free. If one of her workers stole, China Mary paid for it.

In addition to several laundry facilities, China Mary also owned a general store that was typically well stocked with American and Chinese products. She permitted both Chinese and American men to use the gambling hall located in the back of her store as long as they respected her rules. She was also an investor in Sam Sing's popular Chinese restaurant, as well as a pseudo banker for Chinese and white men alike. In fact, if anyone needed just about anything, including food or medical care, they could go to China Mary. Occasionally, China Mary would help pay medical bills for those who could not afford the bills themselves.

China Mary

China Mary died on December 16, 1906 at the age of 65. She was laid to rest in Tombstone's Boothill Cemetery, which got its name thanks to the number of cowboys who died and were buried with their boots on. She was buried near some of Tombstone's other Chinese residents, including a friend named Quong Gu Kee and a candy store owner named Foo Kee, who was killed when he was accidentally stabbed in a brawl between two other men.

Quong Gu Kee was known to be a good manager who took over the Can Can restaurant, converting it into a modern fine dining establishment complete with white tablecloths, sturdy oak chairs, and art on the walls. The food was a mix of American cuisine that the cowboys favored, such as pork, beef, and beans, as well as some Chinese dishes. It was a popular establishment among some of Tombstone's more famous citizens, including Wyatt Earp, Billy Clanton, and Curly Bill Brocious. Quong expressed some sadness when Billy Clanton was killed in the Gunfight at the O.K. Corral, partly because he always paid his bill.

Quong died in Bisbee and was buried there, but he was so popular in Tombstone that his friends paid to have his remains exhumed. Quong was then reinterred at Boothill Cemetery after a large memorial that was presided over by an Episcopal minister. Over 500 people came to pay their respects to Quong, including a senator from Maine, who gave Quong's eulogy.

When the mining boom eased up in the early 20th century, the Chinese population in Tombstone dwindled until it was nearly nonexistent by the 1930s. Some may have gone to Tucson, which had a healthy population of Chinese residents and its own Chinatown until it was demolished in the 1960s.

Chapter 6: The Gunfight at the O.K. Corral

Tombstone was a remarkable place in many ways during the 19th century, but it's altogether possible (if not likely) that Tombstone would have been a historical footnote without the events of October 26, 1881. Much the same way Deadwood is associated with Wild Bill Hickok, Tombstone has become one of the iconic symbols of the Old West because some of the West's biggest legends called it home, and because Tombstone played host to the Gunfight at the O.K. Corral.

In 1878, Wyatt Earp was a 30 year old lawman in Dodge City, Kansas looking for something new in life. He had witnessed the power of wealth each time cattle barons ended their cattle drives in Dodge City, and now he hoped to be able to trade in his badge for the opportunity to make some cash. Wyatt sensed the opportunity had come when his older brother Virgil contacted him about a silver strike in the rugged hills of southern Arizona Territory. Virgil Earp had been living in northern Arizona, serving in various law enforcement roles in the capital of Prescott, and when Virgil was appointed U.S. deputy marshal of Pima County in southern Arizona, he sent for his brothers, Wyatt and Morgan, to serve as special deputies to help him deal with the cowboys. With the lure of striking it rich in the silver mines, Wyatt Earp left Kansas in 1879 for the silver-mining boomtown of Tombstone, Arizona.

Wyatt Earp

Virgil Earp

Of course, Wyatt Earp would become known for everything but being a miner, and sure enough, the Earps were out of the mining business almost as quickly as they attempted to enter it. With no prospects for mining, Wyatt had little choice but to get back into law enforcement, something he had vowed to leave behind. His rather short retirement from law enforcement ended when he accepted a job as shotgun rider for Wells Fargo. Earp's job was to protect the content of the strongbox under the driver's seat. Weighing up to 150 pounds and made of oak, pine, and iron, the strongboxes containing gold, cash, and other valuables were natural targets for thieves. Earp was glad to leave the job in the summer of 1880, and with his other business ventures having already failed so quickly, he became a deputy sheriff of Tombstone. The sheriff was Fred White, the town's first marshal. Despite being on the other side of the law, White got along well with the cowboys he occasionally had to arrest. By all accounts, he was an honest and fair lawman that steered clear of politics.

In September 1880, Wyatt was joined by a man he had met awhile back in Texas, and as fate would have it, they would be eternally associated with each other in history. To a great extent, the lives of Doc Holliday and Wyatt Earp will forever be defined by the Gunfight at the O.K. Corral, which Earp would spend his final years trying to forget. In fact, no stories about Earp in Tombstone are complete without Holliday.

Doc Holliday

Holliday has come to be viewed by many as Earp's sidekick. John Henry "Doc" Holliday was a good friend to Earp and raised to be loyal to his friends, but he was nobody's sidekick. A former dentist who became something of a professional gambler, the eccentric Holliday was considered dangerous and perhaps a little crazy by many. When Dodge City Sheriff Bat Masterson became a writer, he wrote about Holliday, "He was selfish and had a perverse nature – traits not calculated to make a man popular in the early days of the frontier." Holliday had a reputation for a fast draw and a quick temper, and Wyatt Earp later claimed that it was this streak in Holliday that saved his life in 1878 and cemented their friendship.

Earp had invited Holliday to join him in Tombstone, which stayed in Holliday's mind as he gambled and walked the streets of Prescott, Arizona. Prescott, Arizona bore little resemblance to Tombstone. The northern Arizona town was the capital, lost the title to Tucson in 1867, then got it back again in 1877 before losing it for good to Phoenix in 1889. Whether it was due to the end of his hot streak at the tables or due to strong recruitment effort by Wyatt, it was September 1880 when Holliday finally arrived in Tombstone, according to voter registration records. Weeks before he arrived, Tombstone's Oriental Saloon was in business, and it was the most luxurious saloon and gambling hall in the frontier town. When Holliday arrived, the town was experiencing a gambling war between the so-called Easterners, gamblers who came from east of the Pacific Coast, and the Slopers, mostly from California. Wyatt had recently been given an interest in the Oriental's gambling hall, providing him with a cut of the concessions in exchange for helping keep order among the gamblers who hoped to disrupt the town's gambling arrangements.

On October 28, 1880, Tombstone marshal Fred White headed to Allen Street to break up a group of intoxicated men shooting their guns into the air, apparently at the Moon. As White grabbed the pistol of an outlaw cowboy named Curly Bill Brocius, it went off, hitting White in the groin. Wyatt, seeing the start of the confrontation, commandeered someone's pistol and pistol-whipped Curly Bill, all while Curly Bill's friends started shooting at him. White died days later, and even though the Earps likely saved Curly Bill's life by taking him into custody before the mob got hold of him, he remained permanently bitter about being pistol-whipped. He would later be implicated by at least one person in the murder of Morgan Earp in March 1882. Curly Bill became Arizona's most famous outlaw after the shooting of White, but his reign would be short. Less than two years later, Curly Bill would die in a shootout at the hands of none other than Wyatt Earp.

Curly Bill

When the news came from Prescott in Spring 1881 that Tombstone was going to be the seat of Cochise County, Wyatt liked his chances at being named sheriff, which was also a profitable position because the sheriff collected the taxes. Wyatt already had a history of "misusing" funds and having others go missing. He assumed that being from the North would carry some weight with the Republican governor, John C. Fremont, as would the fact that he was more aligned with the town's business interests. But when it became obvious to Earp that Fremont planned to appoint Democrat Johnny Behan, he withdrew from consideration. Earp also claimed that Behan promised to make him the undersheriff, but this never happened.

Behan

Behan was known to associate with the Clanton brothers and the McLaury brothers. Ike and Billy Clanton and Frank and Tom McLaury were cowboys, which raised eyebrows among those who questioned Behan's allegiance to the law. He most likely developed the friendship when he worked at the bar at the Grand Hotel, a favorite cowboy establishment.

Tom McLaury

Frank McLaury

In March 1881, a stagecoach robbery took place outside Tombstone. Sheriff Johnny Behan led one posse, and Virgil Earp led the other. Virgil Earp's posse was a veritable "who's who" of Western lore. In addition to his brothers Morgan and Wyatt, his posse included Doc Holliday, Bat Masterson, as well as Bob Paul and Marshall Williams.

Morgan Earp

During the hunt for the robbers, some remarked that the robbers were "hunting for themselves." The primary target of that remark was Doc Holliday. Will McLaury, a lawyer and brother to Tom and Frank, plainly said that Holliday robbed the Benson stage. To add to the intrigue about Holliday is his girlfriend, "Big Nose" Kate Elder. Kate was also a heavy drinker, and on one occasion, she wandered into a Tombstone saloon after an argument with Holliday. As the whiskey took hold, she began to talk about Holliday to anyone who would listen. She talked about how he treated her and how she believed that much of the abuse she took was because of the influence of the Earps, who she detested. One of the people who happened to be there to hear Kate unload about Holliday was none other than Sheriff Behan. His dislike for Holliday was hardly a secret, and his ears perked up at the possibility that he might actually have something to pin on the eccentric gambler.

In the summer of 1881, Wyatt still hoped to become sheriff, which might happen if he could find the robbers and arrest them. He worked out a deal with Ike Clanton, who was well acquainted with the cowboys that made their way in and out of Tombstone. Earp was confident that the cowboys knew who pulled off the robbery. Wyatt arranged a meeting with Ike, Frank McLaury, and another rancher named Joe Hill at the Oriental Saloon. Wyatt offered each of the men $1,200 of the reward money that Wells Fargo had put up for the capture of the robbers, dead or alive. Of course, Wyatt wanted the credit for it, but he was willing to forgo the reward money. If he was elected sheriff, he stood to make around $30,000 a year because he was also allowed to keep a portion of the taxes he collected.

Billy Leonard, Jim Crane, and Harry Head were in hiding, knowing that they were accused of the stagecoach robbery. Wyatt's plan was to lure them out to the McLaury ranch using fake information about a stagecoach carrying a load of money. Wyatt planned to be there and put the three men under arrest. However, on June 10, Head and Leonard were killed when they were caught trying to steal cattle.

Unfortunately for Ike Clanton, the plan further deteriorated when Marshall Williams, a Wells Fargo agent, had too much to drink and said that Ike Clanton was involved with murders. Clanton, now fearing for his life, was furious with Earp, who he believed would divulge the plan. If any cowboys knew that he had tried to set up Head, Crane, and Leonard, he would be killed. Clanton had insisted that Earp keep quiet about the arrangement, and he now felt that Wyatt betrayed him. Harboring the secret clearly did not ease Clanton's mind; he was convinced that Earp told Holliday about the arrangement, but Earp denied it. Clanton tried to goad Earp into admitting that he told Holliday by saying that Doc himself said he knew about the deal. Holliday was in Tucson when, on October 21, Wyatt sent Morgan to get him and ask him to return to Tombstone. Wyatt wanted to ask Holliday himself what, if anything, he knew. When Holliday arrived, he assured Wyatt he knew nothing about a deal between him and Ike Clanton, who had briefly left town to tend to other business.

Another piece in the puzzle that would result in the famous gunfight fell into place on June 6. Marshal Ben Sippy unexpectedly left Tombstone, saying he needed a two-week leave of absence, and Virgil was left in charge. When Sippy never returned, possibly because he was hiding out from creditors and may have embezzled money from the city, Virgil was named the acting city marshal. Now he and Wyatt both held positions of authority in Tombstone.

Throughout the middle months of 1881, the resentment between the Earps and McLaurys also began to mount. Another stagecoach was robbed near Tombstone on September 8, and this time it was going from Tombstone to Bisbee when two masked bandits robbed the stagecoach and its passengers. As the robbery was in progress, the driver happened to hear one of the bandits refer to the cash tucked away in the Wells Fargo strongbox using law enforcement slang. The money was called "sugar." Frank Stilwell, a former deputy to Sheriff Behan, was named as a suspect. When a boot heel print in the dirt matched one that Stilwell had recently had replaced at a local shoemaker, Stilwell was arrested, as was Pete Spence, his livery stable partner. Stilwell and Spence both happened to be friends with the McLaury brothers, and Wyatt Earp would later testify that the Clantons and the McLaurys were involved in the ambush on the Mexicans and blew the cash on whiskey, women, and cards.

Judge Wells Spicer, who would figure prominently in the aftermath of the Gunfight at the OK Corral, dismissed the charges against Stilwell and Spence due to lack of evidence. Still, many say that the cowboys took the arrest as a personal insult. Frank McLaury reportedly said as much in an argument with Virgil Earp. He also accused Virgil of being part of a vigilante group that was supposedly being formed to lynch the local cowboys. Virgil vehemently denied this and said it was not him but Sheriff Behan that was behind it. In response, Frank told him it made no difference if it was Virgil or Behan who was responsible; either way, he was not going to let them interfere with his life and he would die defending his right to keep his guns if he had to do so. He warned Virgil that there would be retribution for what he felt was unfair harassment of the cowboys.

Wells Spicer

After Stilwell and Spence were released on bail, Virgil Earp arrested the pair again on October 13, either for a different charge or for a different robbery, but the McLaurys believed that Earp was harassing the two and arresting them for the same charge as before. Frank McLaury warned Morgan Earp that if the Earps arrested the McLaurys or their friends again, they were dead men.

Despite that warning, it seems the McLaurys were preparing to leave town in late October. With the perceived threat of a vigilante committee still in the air, they sold off their cattle, and word had it that they were going to stop in Fort Worth, Texas before going to Iowa for the wedding of their sister Sarah.

On October 25, Frank McLaury and Billy Clanton were in the process of rounding up some of the last of their cattle east of Tombstone, and Tom McLaury and Ike Clanton went into town to take care of some business accounts. As he was known to do, Ike started throwing back some whiskey. He was still paranoid about the deal he had made with Wyatt to set up the cowboys who had robbed the Benson stagecoach, and getting drunk did nothing to ease his concerns. Several people said later that they heard Ike make drunken threats against the Earps, and Ike supposedly heard that Holliday was also making accusations against him.

Ike got his chance to confront Holliday directly later that night at a local saloon. Holliday, with Morgan Earp nearby, told Ike that he did not like the things he was hearing Ike say about him and challenged him to a fight. By now, Clanton was extremely drunk and continued his threats. Holliday responded by calling Clanton a liar. The incident was on the verge of escalating into a gunfight when Virgil intervened and threatened to arrest them both. Ike, who was unarmed, backed off and moved on to a poker game. As he turned to go, he asked Doc and Morgan not to shoot him in the back.

Interestingly, two of the other men in the card game Ike joined were Virgil Earp and Johnny Behan. Virgil played cards with his gun in his lap until the game finally broke up at 7:00 a.m. the next morning. In one last drunken burst, Ike told Virgil to tell Holliday that he would get him the next time he saw him. He may also have threatened Wyatt that same night. Virgil later claimed he told Ike to go sleep it off.

When the Earps and Holliday woke up the next morning, October 26, 1882, they were told that Ike Clanton was walking the streets of Tombstone, going from saloon to saloon to announce his intentions to kill them. Some said Clanton went into the telegraph office to wire for help, and the town began to buzz with concern that a gang of angry cowboys was about to descend on Tombstone. Holliday could not help but hear the rumors and went to help. Virgil told him, "This is none of your affair," to which Holliday said, "That is a hell of thing to say to me." After the events that followed, many questioned why Holliday, known to have a quick temper, would be asked to help disarm the Clantons and the McLaurys, if that was Virgil's intention.

Perhaps fueled by courage from the whiskey, Ike managed to locate two guns. He had a revolver and a Winchester rifle with him when he went from saloon to saloon, looking for Holliday and any of the Earp brothers. Virgil was sleeping off his own late night, but he was getting enough warnings about what Ike was up to that he thought it wise to get out of bed and look into the situation. It was not hard to find Ike in his current condition. Virgil snuck up behind him and knocked him in the head with his own revolver. He took Ike's guns and hauled the drunken cowboy into court.

Before the judge could arrive, Wyatt, Virgil, and Morgan Earp got into an argument with Ike. The whole situation nearly ended right then and there when Morgan offered Ike a six-shooter to give him a chance to take his best shot. Deputy Sheriff Dave Campbell intervened, temporarily preventing a gunfight. Ike was fined $25 by the judge and told he could find his guns at the Grand Hotel. It was suggested that he might want to pick up his guns and leave town before he got into more serious trouble.

This did little to ease the tension as far as Wyatt was concerned, and as he left the courtroom, he came across another nemesis, Tom McLaury. More taunts and threats were exchanged, and many who were there say that Wyatt challenged McLaury to a gunfight, but Tom told him he was not going to fight him. As he said to Billy Breakenridge, he was not involved in the feud with the Earps and told Wyatt he had no issue with him. Wyatt responded by slapping McLaury and sending his pistol across the side of McLaury's head. The bloody McLaury fell into the street. Later, Wyatt testified that Tom had challenged him to a draw, which is something that Wyatt could have arrested him for. As is the case with many of the details of this feud, the exact truth may never be known. Regardless of who started it, the encounter only added fuel to the fire. Wyatt also claimed that Tom was intentionally causing a stir by telling Wyatt he was unarmed despite plainly and visibly carrying a revolver tucked near his right hip. It was for this reason that the Earps may have assumed Tom was armed when the gunfight started hours later.

While Ike was causing a stir in Tombstone with his drunken threats, his brother Billy and Tom McLaury's brother Frank were with another rancher named Edwin Frank. Around 2:00 p.m. Billy Clanton, Frank McLaury and Edwin Frank returned to Tombstone after spending the morning east of town rounding up cattle. When they arrived at the Grand Hotel, Billy and Frank were given the update on what their brothers had been up to, prompting them to immediately leave the hotel without even having a drink. They set out to find their brothers and, according to witnesses who were at the hotel, get them out of Tombstone before they got themselves killed. From there, they met up with a man named Billy Claiborne, who had been helping Ike get first aid from the local doctor. The Earps were already worried about rumors that the Clantons and McLaurys were trying to build up a mob to confront them, and the addition of Billy Clanton, Frank McLaury, Edwin Frank and Billy Claiborne would certainly add to that concern, even if it wasn't their intention.

An 1882 picture of the O.K. Corral

Shortly after 2:00, they were all seen around the O.K. Corral, and their next stop was Spangenberg's Gun Shop. Wyatt saw the McLaurys and the Clantons go into the gun shop, which no doubt caught his attention. As he approached the shop, Frank McLaury's horse stepped up onto the sidewalk, which was a violation of a town ordinance. Wyatt grabbed the horse's bridle and was moving him from the sidewalk as Frank came out and jerked the bridle away. Wyatt told him to get his horse off the sidewalk, and Frank did so without incident. As this was going on, Ike Clanton was trying to buy a pistol, but the merchant would not sell him one, most likely due to his drunken condition.

The McLaurys and the Clantons left the shop and the Earps milled around the vicinity of the Oriental Saloon, a favorite stomping ground of Virgil's in particular. Tom McLaury went to Everhardy's Butcher Shop, and everyone else in his gang went to Dexter's Livery to retrieve Billy Clanton's horse. Both the trip to the butcher shop and the livery took the Clantons and the McLaurys in the direction of the O.K. Corral.

Meanwhile, the Earps were discussing what their next move should be. Johnny Behan had been made aware of the growing tension and the threats between the two groups of men as soon as he got out of bed that day. Virgil's version of his meeting with Behan was that he asked Behan if he would help confront the McLaurys and Clantons and disarm them, but Behan refused. Behan later said that when he went to ask Virgil what was going on, Virgil said that the cowboys were looking for a fight and he was going to give them one. Behan said that he reminded Virgil that he was supposed to be keeping the peace, not disturbing it by engaging in gunfights. According to Behan, he then went out toward Fremont Street to talk to the cowboys and take their guns.

After talking to Behan, Virgil grabbed a sawed-off shotgun and met his brothers and Doc Holliday at Hafford's Saloon. Witnesses saw Tom McLaury leave the butcher shop around that same time, obviously trying to conceal something in his pocket. It may have been a gun, but others say it may have been a wad of cash since he was carrying nearly $3,000 on him that afternoon. Tom met up with his brother and the Clantons at the front of the O.K. Corral, walked through it, and went out toward an alley in the back. The McLaurys went off to the Union Market while the Clantons went down the alley toward a vacant lot. Fly's Boarding House and Photography Gallery and Harwood's Boarding House were nearby, on Fremont Street.

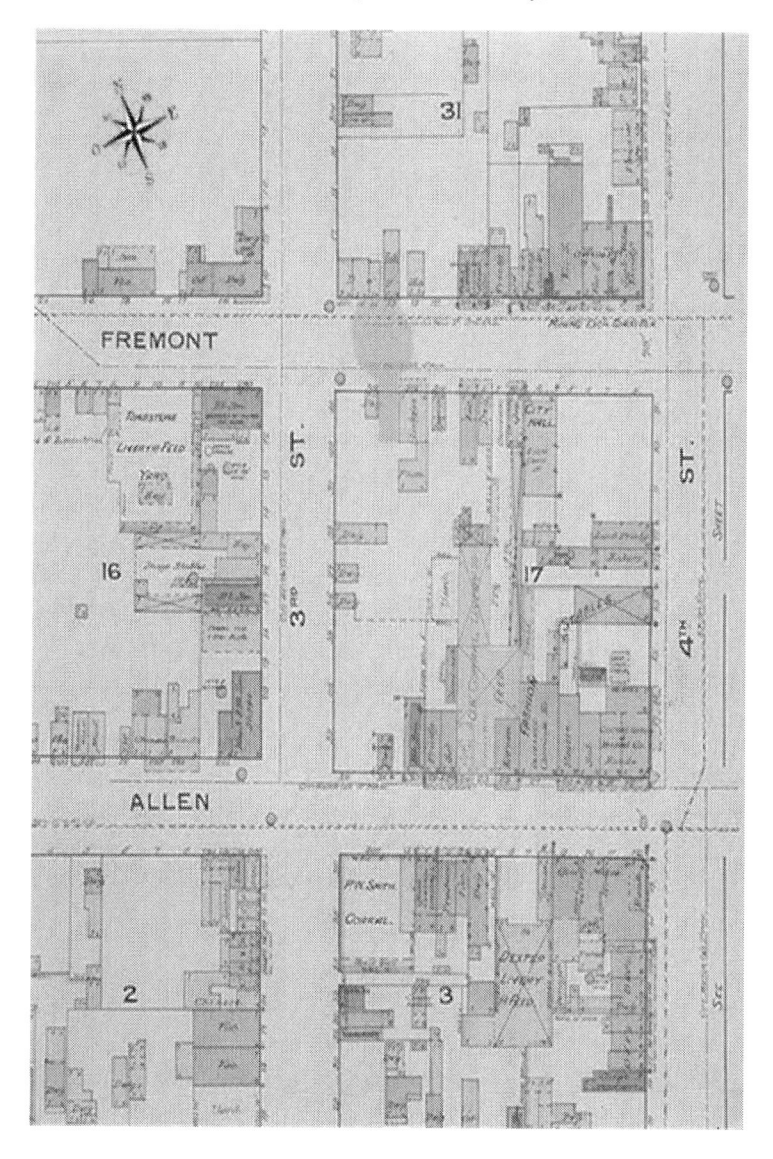

A map of Tombstone. The O.K. Corral is in yellow. The spot of the gunfight is in green.

At that same time, the Earps were walking down Fremont Street, accompanied by Doc Holliday. The Earps were carrying revolvers, while Holliday had a pistol and the sawed off shotgun given to him by Virgil stashed under his coat, presumably to avoid scaring the townspeople. The fact that Holliday was with them does raise questions about Virgil Earp's intentions. If he was, as he later claimed, planning to disarm the cowboys, asking Holliday to help was an odd move. Ever since Holliday had been diagnosed with tuberculosis, he lived his life as if he had nothing to lose and was more than willing to take chances in gunfights.

As the McLaurys were doing business for money owed to them at the Union Market, Johnny Behan found them and tried to disarm them. Frank McLaury told Behan he was not planning to cause any trouble, but he was also not planning to give up his gun. He did not trust the Earps, and after what had already occurred that day, Frank felt that he needed to be able to defend himself if need be.

Behan then went with Frank and Tom McLaury to an empty lot where the Clanton brothers, Billy Claiborne, and another man named Wesley Fuller were waiting. Behan again demanded Frank's gun, as well as Billy's, but both men refused. Behan checked the other men for weapons and determined that they were unarmed, just as the Earps and Holliday came around the corner to Fremont Street. The Earps later claimed Behan told them he had disarmed the cowboys, while Behan claimed he had only told them he had tried to disarm the cowboys, not that he had actually done so. Either way, Behan wisely took cover in the nearby boarding house as the Earps continued walking down Fremont Street. According to Virgil, he was now intent on avoiding a fight because Behan told them the cowboys were disarmed: "I had a walking stick in my left hand and my hand was on my six-shooter in my waist pants, and when he said he had disarmed them, I shoved it clean around to my left hip and changed my walking stick to my right hand." Wyatt claimed he "took my pistol, which I had in my hand, under my coat, and put it in my overcoat pocket."

The McLaurys and Clantons had been conducting business in the shops near where they had congregated around the O.K. Corral, but the Earps and Holliday may have perceived their position as a threat. The group was standing around a vacant lot on Fremont Street near the rear of the O.K. Corral, in close proximity to where Holliday was renting a room and on the route to the homes of the Earps. The Earps and Holliday may have believed they were trying to send a message.

As the Earps made their way to the entrance of the vacant lot, Billy Claiborne and Wesley Fuller backed off, leaving the Earps and Holliday just steps away from the McLaurys and the Clantons. Virgil raised his walking stick and demanded their guns. Holliday stepped up and shoved the shotgun he was carrying into the stomach of one of the cowboys. The next sound everyone heard was the cocking of two pistols, followed by Virgil saying, "Hold, I don't want that!"

Despite the fact that the most famous gunfight in American history took place moments later, exactly how it all went down remains heavily disputed and not completely clear.

The biggest controversy is over who actually started the fight. Those that side with the cowboys say they were ambushed and not even given a chance to defend themselves. Some say that they heard Morgan Earp say that it was time to let the cowboys have it and Holliday agreed. According to their version, the cowboys immediately put their hands up, Morgan Earp fired first, and the Earp gang got off four shots before the armed cowboys could even draw their weapons. Those that side with the Earps claimed that when Virgil told the cowboys to put their hands up, Tom McLaury reached for a rifle in one of the horse's scabbards. It was at that moment that Holliday stuck the gun in Tom's stomach, forcing him to let go of the rifle, and then Holliday stepped back two paces. Then, the two clicks came from guns wielded by Billy Clanton and Frank McLaury. According to this version, Billy shot at Wyatt first, but Wyatt returned fire at Frank because he was considered the most dangerous shooter. The pro-Earp contingent also suggested that Claiborne or Behan was taking shots at the Earps from the photo gallery.

Who started the shooting was disputed, but everyone agreed that two shots were fired almost simultaneously, touching off the firing (Virgil later claimed at least one of these shots came from Billy Clanton). The small space was filled with gunfire as 30 shots flew in a span of just 30 seconds.

Frank McLaury took the first bullet in his right side before falling onto Fremont Street. Witnesses said Frank started staggering to the ground in the middle of the street while trying to pull a rifle out of a scabbard attached to a horse. Either Frank or Billy Clanton then shot Morgan Earp in the shoulder. As he fell to the ground, Morgan took another shot at Frank.

Although the Earps believed Tom McLaury was unarmed, he was near a horse, possibly trying to get a rifle. Virgil and Wyatt later claimed they saw Tom covering himself with the horse and moving himself as the horse moved, hiding behind it and firing at least once over the horse's back. Whether Tom fired at all is unclear, because Holliday blasted him in the chest with the shotgun in just a few seconds. Tom fell near a pole at the corner of 3rd Street and Fremont Street, mortally wounded and out of the gunfight. Holliday then dropped the shotgun and pulled out his pistol and kept firing.

At some point in the firing, Ike Clanton ran up to Wyatt and grabbed his arm, saying he did not have a gun. Wyatt shoved him away and said, "The fight has commenced. Go to fighting or get away." With that, Ike ran off to Fly's boarding house.

Billy Clanton continued to fight while he lay wounded in the street. Shot in the chest and right wrist, his body already riddled by seven bullet wounds, he was able to push himself up against a wall and shot at Virgil with his left hand, piercing Virgil's calf with a bullet. Billy called for more bullets, even as he was dying. Frank also continued to fight, staggering across the street to take aim at Holliday. Frank allegedly said to Holliday, "I've got you now," to which Holliday supposedly replied, "You're a daisy if you do." A shot hit Holliday in the hip, incensing him and leading him to chase after Frank shouting, "That son of a bitch has shot me, and I am going to kill him." At this point, Frank was stumbling around the street and was an easy mark for Morgan and Holliday, who simultaneously took aim at him and blasted him in the head and chest.

Just like that, it was over. People began to emerge onto the street when the shooting stopped. C.S. Fly, the boardinghouse and photo gallery owner, took Billy Clanton's gun and ignored his request for more bullets to continue the fight. Another group of men pulled Holliday away from Frank McLaury's dead body. Holliday was still so enraged about McLaury shooting him that he wanted to put a couple more bullets into him for good measure. Tom McLaury was still breathing when he was pulled from the street, but he died within the hour. Dr. William Millar examined Billy Clanton when he was taken to Fly's, and after determining he could do nothing for him, Dr. Millar filled him with morphine so he could die in peace. As he was being taken to Fly's, Billy was telling anyone who could hear him, "They have murdered me. I have been murdered. Chase the crowd away and from the door and give me air."

However it had happened, the Gunfight at the O.K. Corral resulted in an unarmed Ike Clanton and Billy Claiborne running away while the McLaury brothers, including an unarmed Tom, were dead in the street. Billy Clanton had suffered a painful and fatal gunshot wound to the chest, while Virgil Earp, Morgan Earp and Doc Holliday were all wounded. It is believed that Billy Clanton and Frank McLaury, even after being wounded, continued shooting, and one of them hit Morgan Earp across the back. Wyatt managed to walk away without so much as a scratch. According to Big Nose Kate, Holliday was openly weeping when he came back to his room, crying, "That was awful, awful."

Moments after the gunfight, the man who had instigated the whole incident, Ike Clanton, was located in a dance hall and arrested. It was probably safer for him in a jail cell than on the street anyway. After Virgil and Morgan were loaded onto a wagon and taken home, Doc and Wyatt remained out on Fremont Street. As they were discussing the events, Sheriff Behan approached Wyatt and told him he was under arrest. Wyatt told Behan that Behan had lied to him when he said that all of the men were unarmed, and that he was not going to be arrested. Several of the local citizens came to Wyatt's defense and said there was no reason to arrest him. Some say that Behan seemed more than a little intimidated by Wyatt. Whether it was out of fear or the fact that Wyatt talked him out of it, Behan let Wyatt go.

For a while, the Earps were considered heroes. The local newspapers agreed that they had no choice but to fire when Frank McLaury fired on them first. *The Tombstone Epitaph*'s described the shootout, "Wyatt Earp stood up and fired in rapid succession, as cool as a cucumber, and was not hit." The *San Francisco Examiner* suggested that Tombstone's residents should be grateful to have the Earps on their side of the law.

The *Epitaph* in particular had a great deal of coverage of the gunfight, including the events leading up to it. The following day, it reported:

"Stormy as were the early days of Tombstone, nothing ever occurred equal to the event of yesterday. Since the Retirement of Ben Sippy as marshal and the appointment of V.W. Earp to fill the vacancy, the town has been noted for its quietness and good order. The fractious and much dreaded cowboys, when they came to town, were on their good behavior and no unseemly brawls were indulged in, and it was hoped by our citizens that no more such deeds would occur as led to the killing of Marshal White one year ago. This time it struck with its full and awful force upon those who, heretofore, have made the good name of this county a by word and a reproach, instead of upon some officer in the discharge of his duty of a peaceable and unoffending citizen."

Since the arrest of Stilwell and Spencer for the robbery of the Bisbee stage, there have been oft repeated threats conveyed to the Earp brothers - Virgil, Wyatt, and Morgan - that the friends of the accused, or in other words, the cowboys, would get even with them for the part they have taken in the pursuit and arrest of Stilwell and Spencer. The active part of the Earps in going after stage robbers, beginning with the one last spring where Budd Philpot lost his life, and the more recent one near Contention, has made them exceedingly obnoxious to the bad element of this county and put their lives in jeopardy every month.

Sometime Tuesday, Ike Clanton came into town and during the evening had some little talk with Doc Holliday and Marshal Earp but nothing to cause either to suspect, further than their general knowledge of the man and the threats that had previously been conveyed to the Marshal, that the gang intended to clean out the Earps, that he was thirsting for blood at this time with one exception and that was that Clanton told the Marshal, in answer to a question, that the McLaurys were in Sonora. Shortly after this occurrence someone came to the Marshal and told him that the McLaurys had been seen a short time before just below town. Marshal Earp, now knowing what might happen and feeling his responsibility for the peace and order of the city, stayed on duty all night and added to the police force his brother, Morgan, and Holliday. The night passed without any disturbance whatever and at sunrise he went home and retired to rest and sleep. A short time afterwards one of his officers, named Bronk, came to his house and told him that Clanton was hunting him with threats of shooting him on sight. He discredited the report and did not get out of bed. Sometime later he dressed and went with his brother Morgan uptown. It was not long before another man, Lynch, reported to him the same thing. They walked down Alien Street to Fifth, crossed over to

Fremont and down to Fourth, where, upon turning up Fourth toward Alien, they came upon Clanton with a Winchester rifle in his hand and a revolver on his hip. The marshal walked up to him, grabbed the rifle and hit him a blow on the head at the same time, stunning him so that he was able to disarm him without further trouble. He marched Clanton off to the police court, fined Clanton $25 and costs making $27.50 altogether. This occurrence must have been about 1 o'clock in the afternoon."

The Epitaph continued with an account by an eyewitness named R.F. Coleman:

"I was in the O.K. Corral at 2:30 P.M. when I saw the two Clantons (Ike and Bill) and the two McLaurys (Frank and Tom) in an earnest conversation across the street in Dunbar's Corral. I went up the street and notified Sheriff Behan and told him it was his duty, as sheriff, to go and disarm them. I told him they had gone to the West End Corral. I then went and saw Marshal Virgil Earp and notified him to the same effect. I then met Billy Alien and we walked through the O.K. Corral, about fifty yards behind the sheriff. On reaching Fremont Street I saw Virgil Earp, Wyatt Earp, Morgan Earp, and Doc Holliday, in the center of the street, all armed. I had reached Bauer's Meat Market. Johnny Behan had just left the cowboys, after having a conversation with them. I went along to Fly's Photograph Gallery, when I heard Virgil Earp say, 'Give up your arms or throw up your hands!' there was some reply made by Frank McLaury, when firing became general, over thirty shots being fired. Tom McLaury fell first, but raised and fired again before he died. Bill Clanton fell next, and raised to fire again when Mr. Fly took his revolver from him. Frank McLaury ran a few yards and fell, Morgan Earp was shot through and fell. Doc Holliday was hit in the left hip, but kept firing. Virgil Earp was hit in the third or fourth fire, in the leg which staggered him, but he kept up his effective work. Wyatt Earp stood up and fired in rapid succession, as cool as a cucumber, and was not hit. Doc Holliday was as calm as though at target practice and fired rapidly. After the firing was over, Sheriff Behan went up to Wyatt Earp and said, 'I'll have to arrest you.' Wyatt replied, 'I won't be arrested today. I am right here and I'm not going away. You have deceived me. You told me these men were disarmed! I went to disarm them.'"

As it turned out, Coleman was only in position to see the fighting on Fremont St. and thus was not the best eyewitness. He also had a reputation for exaggerating the story, and he would subsequently tell contradictory accounts. The *Epitaph* concluded:

"This ends Mr. Coleman's story which in the most essential particulars has been confirmed by others. Marshal Earp says that he and his party met the Clantons and the McLaurys in the alleyway by the McDonald place; he called to them to throw up their hands, that he had come to disarm them. Instantaneously Bill Clanton and one of the McLaury's fired, and then it became general. Mr. Earp says it was the first shot from

Frank McLaury that hit him. (Note that Virgil said that Frank McLaury shot him and he should know better than anyone. The only other candidate to have shot him was Billy Clanton. Had Billy shot him from his position his shin bone would have been shattered. The shot had to have come from the side to wound Virgil in such a manner and Frank was the only one in that position.) In other particulars his statement does not materially differ from the statement given. Ike Clanton was not armed and ran across to Alien Street and took refuge in the dance hall there. The two McLaurys and Bill Clanton all died within a few minutes after being shot. The Marshal was shot through the calf of his right leg, the ball going clear through. His brother Morgan, was shot through the shoulders, the ball entering the point of the right shoulder blade, following across the back, shattering off a piece of one vertebrae and passing out the left shoulder in about the same position that it entered the right. (Note that the path of the bullet was in a horizontal path. That means that the only per son that could have shot him was Tom McLaury - across his saddle. Both Billy Clanton and Frank McLaury were in a position such that their shots would have followed a trajectory of an upward angle - not horizontal.) The wound is dangerous but not necessarily fatal, and Virgil's is far more painful than dangerous. Doc Holliday was hit upon the scabbard of his pistol, the leather breaking the force of the ball so that no material damage was done other than to make him limp a little in his walk."

Although the papers mostly sided with the Earps and Holliday, the local undertakers made a different type of statement. The bodies of Billy Clanton, Frank McLaury and Tom McLaury were put on display in the window of Ritter and Ream. Below the coffins that held the deceased cowboys was a sign that read "Murdered in the Streets of Tombstone."

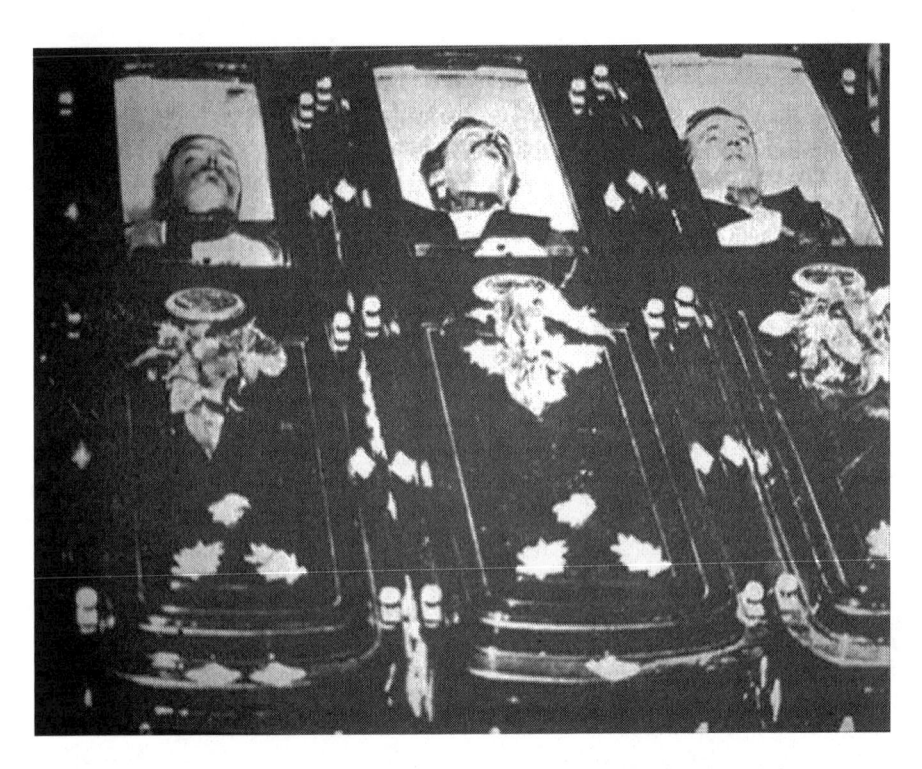

(L-R) The bodies of Tom McLaury, Frank McLaury, and Billy Clanton on display.

The funeral procession was held later that day and was led by the Tombstone Brass Band, which was followed by horses carrying the coffins. Nearly 300 people and 25 wagons and carriages fell in behind, spanning two blocks as they made their way to the graveyard at Boothill Cemetery. Perhaps as many as 3,000 people watched Billy Clanton be laid to rest next to his father, Old Man Clanton, who had died only weeks earlier. Frank and Tom McLaury shared the same grave next to Billy's. Among those that went to Tombstone on the 27th was Will McLaury, older brother to Frank and Tom, who had received a telegraph message informing him of the death of his brothers. He had only recent lost his wife Lona, and now he was forced to leave his young son and daughter behind in Texas with family friends to tend to business in Tombstone.

The graves of Billy, Frank and Tom at Boothill Cemetery in Tombstone

On Friday, October 28, the inquest called by H.M. Matthews had begun. Ike Clanton filed murder charges against Holliday and the Earps. As suspected, Matthews reported that Billy, Frank, and Tom had died due to gunshot wounds from the Earp brothers and Holliday. The Tombstone Nugget reported on Dr. Matthews' testimony:

"...they (the McLaurys and Clanton) died from the affects of pistol and gunshot wounds; there were two wounds on the body (Clanton); did not examine them thoroughly; there was one two inches from the left nipple, penetrating the lungs; the other was beneath the twelfth rib, above and beneath, six inches to the right of the navel; think neither of the wounds went through the body; not probing the wounds, cannot positively say what direction they took; both were in front through the body; my opinion at that time was that those wounds were the cause of death; examined the body of Frank McLaury at the same time and day; found in the body of Frank McLaury one wound, penetrating the abdomen one inch to the left of the navel...I examined the body of Tom McLaury at the same time and place; found on his body twelve buckshot wounds - on the right side of the body, near together, under the arms, between the third and fifth ribs; my opinion was that they were buckshot wounds; laid the palm of my hand on them; it would cover the whole of them, about four inches in space..."

A hearing was scheduled for the following week on November 1. Even with the typical violence and gunplay that came with mining towns like Tombstone, this incident weighed heavy on the minds of many locals. It was not long before people took sides, often changing sides by the hour, depending on what tidbit of information they had heard that day. Wyatt and Doc spent 16 days in jail, while Virgil Earp was temporarily suspended as town marshal.

Judge Wells Spicer presided over the Earp/Holliday inquest hearing. The Earps had retained Thomas Fitch as their defense attorney, and Thomas J. Drum defended Doc Holliday. The new district attorney, Lyttleton Price, and Benjamin Goodrich, the attorney for Ike Clanton, led the prosecution. The defense attorneys asked that the defendants be allowed to remain out of jail. Spicer agreed to $10,000 for each man, which was raised and paid by the defense attorneys and a witness for the defense. Will McLaury, who arrived in Tombstone on November 3rd, was quite surprised to see Wyatt Earp walking the streets, gun strapped to his hip, when he was the subject of a coroner's inquest. Will was also curious to know what had happened to $1,600 of the $3,000 that his brother Tom had in his possession when he died.

Attorney Thomas Fitch

An attorney himself, Will joined the prosecution team the next morning. He immediately asked that bail be revoked, even though Price and Goodrich had warned him not to do that. Doing so might only serve to make the Earps even angrier than they already were, but Will said he was not the least bit afraid of Wyatt Earp or Doc Holliday. He wanted justice for the death of his brothers. Judge Spicer had a change of heart about the bail and on November 7, Wyatt and Doc were put in jail. With Morgan and Virgil still recuperating from their gunshot wounds, nobody was worried that they would try and leave town. According to Will, getting Wyatt and Doc off the streets relieved the tension that had been in the air since before the shooting. He took it as a sign that Wyatt and Doc deserved no less than death by hanging.

The prosecutors made their case that the Earps and Holliday had planned to murder the Clantons and the McLaurys all along. They brought in witnesses who swore that the dead men were trying to surrender when they were killed. Johnny Behan testified for the prosecution and said that he ordered Virgil stay out of a fight with the cowboys. Ike Clanton told the court that the deal that went bad with Wyatt over the attempt to capture the stagecoach robbers compelled Wyatt to want to commit murder.

Several witnesses called by the prosecutors claimed the Earps or Holliday fired first, including Behan. However, Behan testified that the first shot came from Holliday's pistol, and it's known that Holliday killed Tom McLaury with a shotgun blast seconds into the fight. As one author points out, for Behan's testimony to be accepted, " the court would have to believe that Holliday marched down Fremont Street carrying a shotgun; put it aside in order to pull out his pistol; fired the first shot, presumably at Billy Clanton; and then picked up the shotgun in order to kill Tom McLaury—all in the space of a few seconds."

Another witness claimed Billy Clanton tried to avoid fighting near the start and cried out, "Don't shoot me. I don't want to fight." Others say Tom McLaury even threw up his hands as though he was surrendering before the gunfight started. Billy Claiborne testified, "They came within ten feet of where we were standing. When they got to the corner of Fly's building, they had their six-shooters in their hands, and Marshal Earp said, 'You sons-of-bitches, you've been looking for a fight, and you can have it!'"

The attorneys for the defense pointed out that several of the witnesses for the prosecution were criminals and hardly of upstanding character. Predictably, they claimed the cowboys started the whole thing, and that when they were the aggressors against the Earps and Holliday, their clients had no choice but to respond. In fact, it was their duty to respond. Wyatt and Virgil Earp both testified that Ike was furious that the deal he had with Wyatt had gone bad, and that Billy Clanton and Frank McLaury had fired the first shots in the gunfight. The defense found another witness to corroborate that story, even though the witness was nearly 200 feet away from the gunfight.

One witness whose testimony may have swayed the court was H.F. Sills, who testified, "I saw four or five men standing in front of the O. K. Corral on October 26th, about two o'clock in the afternoon, talking of some trouble they had had with Virgil Earp, and they made threats at the time that on meeting him they would kill him on sight. Some one of the party spoke up at the time and said: "That they would kill the whole party of Earps when they met them." I then walked up the street and made inquiry as to who Virgil Earp and the Earps were. A man on the street pointed out Virgil Earp to me and told me he was the city marshal. I went over and called him one side, and told him of the threats that I had overheard this party make. One of the men that made the threats had a bandage around his head at the time, and the day of the funeral he was pointed out to me as Isaac Clanton…[I saw] the marshal go up and speak to this other party. I ... saw them pull out their revolvers immediately. The marshal had a cane in his right hand at the time. He throwed up his hand and spoke. I did not hear the words though. By that time Billy Clanton and Wyatt Earp had fired their guns off."

The residents of Tombstone were fairly divided on who was to blame. This was noted by Clara Spalding Brown, a correspondent for a bunch of California newspapers. She wrote, "Opinion is pretty divided as to the justification of the killing. You may meet one man who will support the Earps, and declare that no other course was possible to save their own lives, and the next man is just as likely to assert that there was no occasion whatever for bloodshed, and that this will be 'a warm place' for the Earps hereafter. At the inquest yesterday, the damaging fact was ascertained that only two of the cowboys were armed, it thus being a most unequal fight." The case even caught the attention of Governor John C. Fremont, who noted, "Many of the very best law-abiding and peace-loving citizens have no confidence in the willingness of the civil officers to pursue and bring to justice that element of out-lawry so largely disturbing the sense of security…[The opinion] is quite prevalent that the civil officers are quite largely in league with the leaders of this disturbing and dangerous element."

After hearing the evidence, Judge Spicer determined that the defendants had acted lawfully and that they should not stand trial for murder, but that the grand jury could still determine otherwise. Even though Tom McLaury was unarmed, Frank McLaury and Billy Clanton were armed, and Ike Clanton had been threatening the Earps and Holliday the night before. Judge Spicer noted:

> "Witnesses for the prosecution state unequivocally that William Clanton fell or was shot at the first fire and Claiborne says he was shot when the pistol was only about a foot from his belly. Yet it is clear that there were no powder burns or marks on his clothes. And Judge Lucas says he saw him fire or in the act of firing several times before he was shot, and he thinks two shots afterwards…
>
> In view of these controversies between Wyatt Earp and Isaac Clanton and Thomas McLaury, and in further view of this quarrel the night before between Isaac Clanton and J. H. Holliday, I am of the opinion that the defendant, Virgil Earp, as chief of police, subsequently calling upon Wyatt Earp, and J. H. Holliday to assist him in arresting and disarming the Clantons and McLaurys—committed an injudicious and censurable act, and although in this he acted incautiously and without due circumspection, yet when we consider the condition of affairs incidental to a frontier

country, the lawlessness and disregard for human life; the existence of a law-defying element in our midst; the fear and feeling of insecurity that has existed; the supposed prevalence of bad, desperate and reckless men who have been a terror to the country, and kept away capital and enterprise, and considering the many threats that have been made against the Earps. I can attach no criminality to his unwise act. In fact, as the result plainly proves, he needed the assistance and support of staunch and true friends, upon whose courage, coolness and fidelity he could depend, in case of an emergency."

Two weeks later, the grand jury upheld Spicer's decision, and the case against the Earps and Doc Holliday was officially closed.

Chapter 7: Revenge

The Earps and Holliday were officially off the hook, but the blood feud was far from finished. The ruling incensed many people in Tombstone and left Ike Clanton still wanting revenge. Any thoughts that the Earps and Holliday were heroes had vanished, and rumors began that the Earps were on a list of men targeted for assassination. The so-called "list" also included Judge Spicer, the mayor, and the prosecution team.

Mayor John Clum was the first to be shot at, presumably by cowboys out for revenge. Shots were fired on a stagecoach on December 14 as Clum was on his way to Washington to take a position as a federal Indian agent. Realizing that he was the target of the bandits, Clum jumped out of the stagecoach to protect the other passengers from further harm. Clum borrowed a horse and eventually made it to Washington unscathed.

Judge Spicer received a letter signed "A Miner." The letter advised him to leave Tombstone or die. Spicer wrote a response that was published in the December 15, 1881 edition of the *Epitaph*, which said he would not succumb to threats by the town's riff raff.

The same night that Spicer's letter was published, Virgil got into an argument with M.E. Joyce at the Oriental. Virgil slapped Joyce when he suggested that he had something to do with Clum nearly getting killed. As Joyce left, he backed out the door, saying he would not want to get killed by the Earps' favorite method – a shot in the back.

Two weeks later, on December 28, Virgil was shot as he exited the Oriental. The shot had come from across the street. A drugstore that was under construction had provided good cover for the shooter, who was never caught. Ike Clanton, Curly Bill Brocius, and Will McLaury were the prime suspects. The shot had torn into Virgil's arm, spinning him around. He kept his feet until collapsing into Wyatt's arms when he found him down the street. Virgil permanently lost use of his arm and struggled with the injury for the rest of his life.

The shooter was never identified, but Ike Clanton's hat was found near where the shots had been fired. Clanton was later acquitted after several eyewitnesses testified he was not in

Tombstone at the time of the shooting. In response to the attack on Virgil, Wyatt requested from the U.S. Marshal Crawley Dake that he be appointed a deputy U.S. marshal and given the ability to choose his own deputies, a request that was granted. The Earps racked up such expenses while bolstering their protection and swelling their ranks that Wyatt later had to mortgage his own house, and it was foreclosed on after he failed to repay the debt.

A few months after the attempt on Virgil's life, the Earps' luck ran out. On March 17, 1882, the Earps were at Schieffelin Hall enjoying a show. When it ended, Morgan and Wyatt decided to go play pool at Hatch's Billiard Hall. As Morgan stood with his back to the door, waiting for his turn to play, a volley of gunfire came in through the window on the door. A bullet struck Morgan in the back, and two others slammed into the wall just above Wyatt's head. Morgan fell to the floor mortally wounded. As the gunmen escaped into the night, Morgan died within the hour. The always well-dressed Doc Holliday reportedly provided the suit for Morgan's burial.

Now it was the Earps and Holliday's turn to seek revenge. Two days after Morgan's death, which happened to be Wyatt's 34th birthday, the grieving Wyatt made arrangements for Morgan's body to be sent to their father's home in Colma, California. Virgil and his wife Allie left for San Francisco under the watchful eye of armed guards, and Holliday joined Wyatt when it was time for Virgil and Allie to board the train from Tucson to San Francisco.

As the train left the station in Tucson, Wyatt claimed to have seen Ike Clanton and Frank Stilwell lying in wait for Virgil. After a brief chase, Clanton got away, but Wyatt shot and killed Stilwell, leaving his body riddled with bullets by the railroad tracks. Though it was just days after the attack on Morgan, Wyatt may already have believed that Stilwell was one of the men who shot at Morgan. Pete Spence's wife later claimed that Spence and Stilwell were among a group of men who had returned home shortly after Morgan had been shot, and that Spence had threatened to harm her if she told authorities anything.

With the financial backing of local businessmen, Wyatt formed a posse with his brother Warren and Holliday to hunt down Morgan's killers. But as the Earps were planning out their revenge, Johnny Behan formed a posse to search for Wyatt, who was now wanted for the murder of Frank Stilwell. Just before conducting his infamous month long "vendetta ride", Wyatt had a famous confrontation with Behan, who sought to meet with him. Wyatt warned the sheriff, "Johnny, if you're not careful you'll see me once too often."

Before Behan's posse could find Wyatt and his posse, the vendetta posse killed a cowboy named Florentino Cruz, also known as Indian Charlie, based on a rumor that he was involved in killing Morgan. Wyatt killed him based on the rumor alone. Soon thereafter, the posse killed Curley Bill Brocius, Wyatt's nemesis from a few years earlier, though there was no evidence that Bronchus was involved with Morgan's death. The lawless vendetta to avenge the killing of

Morgan quickly erased any support Wyatt may have had from the residents or businesses of Tombstone. The funding for his posse quickly dried up.

By the time the Earp Vendetta Ride was over, the posse had killed four outlaws, but there's no hard evidence that any of them had anything to do with Morgan's murder. Wanted for murder, and with little to no support from Tombstone, it was time for Earp and Holliday to leave Arizona. On April 13, 1882, Wyatt Earp and Sadie Marcus left Arizona and went to Gunnison, Colorado to ride out the storm. Wyatt expected the same businessmen who had financed him on his "Vendetta Ride" to come through and work out a pardon for the crimes he had committed so he could return to Tombstone and run for sheriff. However, by this time many in Tombstone were glad to have him gone, and after six months of waiting it was apparent that a pardon would never come. Earp went west again and headed to San Francisco. He never returned to Tombstone.

Wyatt also had to bid farewell to Holliday, and they would never see each other again either. Holliday could not have returned to Arizona if he wanted to, at least not without facing a possible death sentence, but when he arrived in Denver in May 1882, he was arrested for Stilwell's murder. Behan made it clear that if Holliday appeared back in Tombstone, he would see to it that Holliday hanged and called for his extradition back to Arizona. With some intervention from Wyatt, who called on his old friend Bat Masterson (now the sheriff of Trinidad, Colorado) Holliday's extradition to Tombstone was blocked. Masterson had pulled some political strings, which evidently went as high as the governor's office.

The seminal moments associated with Holliday were now behind him, but Holliday's final years were marked by much of the same events as the prior 15 years of his life. He followed the gambling circuit around Colorado as his health permitted, never quite able to escape his reputation or bloodshed. Holliday and Wyatt were falsely accused of killing the cowboy Johnny Ringo, a friend of Ike Clanton's and Frank Stilwell's, in Arizona, but neither men were anywhere near the state at the time. It's possible that Doc was implicated simply because of the bad blood that previously existed between him and Ringo. In Tombstone in January 1882, only 3 months after the Shootout at the O.K. Corral, Holliday got into a heated argument with Ringo and allegedly said, "All I want of you is ten paces out in the street." A duel was stopped only by Tombstone's police, who arrested both of them.

The altitude of Colorado was not good for a man with tuberculosis, and any gains Holliday made in his battle against the disease in New Mexico and Arizona were soon wiped away in the Rocky Mountains. Despite being in his 30s, his hair was graying and his body was wasting away. Holliday relied on a growing dependence on alcohol to ease his misery. On the morning of November 8, 1887, Doc Holliday died at the Glenwood Hotel in Colorado at the age of 36. Legend had it that as he lay dying, Holliday looked at his feet, presumably amused that he was dying with his boots off. For one of the West's most notorious gunslingers, Holliday and countless others probably assumed that he would "die with his boots on" in a gunfight. According to this legend, the nurses said that his last words were, "Damn, this is funny." Given his illness, however, modern historians believe Holliday would've been incapable of speaking coherently in his final days. It was also widely believed that Wyatt was there when Doc died, but Wyatt would not actually hear about his death for months. And even though Big Nose Kate later claimed to have been there, most accounts say Holliday was alone when he died.

By the time Holliday died, Ike Clanton had died earlier that same year in Springerville when a lawman pursuing him on cattle rustling charges shot him out of his saddle. Virgil became a lawman again in the boomtown of Goldfield, Nevada. He died there in 1905 after contracting pneumonia.

The last remaining survivor, Wyatt Earp, became a household name and a national celebrity. Those 30 seconds, which he spent much of the rest of his life trying to forget, made him – and the Gunfight at the O.K. Corral – legendary. Even those who claim no interest in the Wild West have heard of Earp and know about the gunfight on Fremont Street. The gunfight has become part of American mythology. As for Earp, he would have a taste of the newly forming movie industry before he died. Upon meeting Charlie Chaplin in 1914, arguably the most famous man in the world at the time, Chaplin said, "You're the bloke from Arizona, aren't you? Tamed the baddies, huh?"

As late as 1922, Earp was still the subject of scathing newspaper articles. *Los Angeles Times* reporter J.M. Scanland's story about Earp's days as a lawman, titled "Lurid Trails are Left by Olden Day Bandits," had at least one glaring error: it said that Earp was dead. Sadie was furious at the slanted article and contacted the *Times* to tell them so. Earp took it a step further two years later and went to the reporter's home to confront him, resulting in an effusive verbal and written apology.

Still, Earp wanted to more fully clear his name. John Flood and Earp met in 1905 and Flood, an engineer, became Earp's personal secretary. Flood made an attempt at writing the biography, but he was an engineer, not a writer. His manuscript was simply not well written. Sadie and Wyatt asked Hart to use his connections to help get the book published, but even a Hollywood heavyweight like Hart had no luck. Rejection letters came in with every attempt at publication, starting with a query to the *Saturday Evening Post* to see if the magazine was interested in serializing Earp's story. The feedback Earp and Hart received criticized both the content and the style of the manuscript. One publisher simply said that the story was not interesting.

Wyatt Earp had a reputation, and many in the West knew of him, but he was not actually famous when he died in 1929, let alone the household name that he is today. Even among those who knew who he was, it is not likely that anyone other than his wife and past girlfriends really knew Wyatt, other than tales about the 30 second gunfight in Tombstone, which itself had been largely forgotten decades earlier.

Chapter 8: The End of Tombstone's Glory Years

Even though the legend of Tombstone has lived on well into the 21st century, the glory years of Tombstone spanned a relatively brief period of time. The town reached its peak of growth in 1883, with anywhere between 7,000-12,000 residents in Tombstone at a time. Tombstone's mines were producing over $2.5 million worth of gold and silver, and churches and schools were being built. Women and children were now a common sight, and despite the troubles associated with the Earps in 1881, Tombstone appeared to be more than just a town that existed to serve the miners.

However, there were changes in the air that led to Tombstone's decline. One major change was in the United States monetary system. As silver was phased out, the price of silver dropped. This led to a drop in wages for the mining industry, and that set off a period of labor unrest in Tombstone. The financial situation was further complicated in 1884 by the failure of the Safford Hudson Bank of Tucson, which had a branch in Tombstone. With it went the savings of many of the area's miners, who were intent on taking their anger out on the mining companies by destroying equipment until a band of soldiers from Fort Huachuca and local deputies stepped in to stop the riot.

The worst problems came in 1880 when the Toughnut mine had its first episode of water seepage. Striking water meant that it was only a matter of time before the mines flooded, and mining operations would have to stop unless the water could be pumped out. The following year, miners in the Sulphuret mine hit water at about the 520-foot level. The year after that, in 1882, workers in the Grand Central mine struck water at 620 feet. Most of the miners were experienced enough to know that this was just the beginning, and they were right.

The mining companies brought in engines to help pump water out of the mines, and that worked for a time. By February 1884, over 576,000 gallons of water were being pumped out of the mines every 24 hours. However, the pumping system burned in May 1886, and after that the price of silver fell to 90 cents an ounce. Workers were laid off, and many of those who had not already moved on when the flooding began left Tombstone. Even when the mines began to produce again, it was never the same as it was at the beginning of the 1880s. Tombstone's days as a cosmopolitan Western town were finished.

Chapter 9: The Legends and Legacy

Tombstone's place in American memory may also have been finished if it had not been permanently associated with the Gunfight at the O.K. Corral. After Wyatt Earp's death, writer Stuart Lake moved forward with publishing Earp's biography, a flattering, semi-fictional account of Earp's life titled *Wyatt Earp: Frontier Marshal*. Published in 1931, Earp's biography was not the first one to offer a sensationalized account of Earp's life. Walter Burns called Earp "The Lion of Tombstone" in his 1927 book, *Tombstone, An Iliad of the Southwest*, a publication that Earp feared would interfere with his attempts to get his own book in print. Years later, Stuart Lake admitted to fabricating several of the quotes he attributed to Earp.

Despite the inaccuracies, *Wyatt Earp: Frontier Marshal* set the wheels in motion for the birth of the legendary, even if inaccurate, Wyatt Earp. A glimpse of this was seen shortly before Earp died. The 1928 movie *In Old Arizona* was the first Western talkie, and it featured Warner Baxter as Sergeant Mickey Dunn, who is charged with finding the robber of a Tombstone stagecoach. Raoul Welsh directed the film, and the character of Dunn drew from Earp's life. It also marked the introduction of the singing cowboy, which became a popular movie attraction.

This was followed by numerous characters in books, movies, and television that were either loosely or closely based on Earp. As would be expected, the Gunfight at the O.K. Corral made great movie fodder, starting with 1932's *Law and Order*. The film gave an account of the Gunfight at the O.K. Corral and was based on the novel *Saint Johnson*, written by W.R. Burnett. The Earp character is named Frame Johnson and was first played by John Huston. In the remake in 1953, the future president, Ronald Reagan, portrayed Johnson. In 1934, Lake's book was made into the movie, "Frontier Marshal," this time with the name Michael Earp in place of Wyatt. The name Wyatt Earp was finally used in film in 1942 in *Tombstone*, featuring another retelling of the gunfight in Tombstone. Acting legend Henry Fonda played Wyatt in the 1953 film *My Darling Clementine*.

Earp and Tombstone made it to television in 1955, when Westerns were all the rage. Hugh O'Brien played Earp in the ABC series, "The Life and Legend of Wyatt Earp," which aired until 1961. Joel McRae took his turn at playing Wyatt in the movie *Wichita* in 1955, and 1957's *Gunfight at the O.K. Corral* was nominated for two Academy Awards.

Ultimately, Americans have remembered the Earps, Doc Holliday, the Gunfight at the O.K. Corral and Tombstone itself as a mixture of facts, myths, and legends. The Earps and Holliday continue to be portrayed as heroes of the West, despite the fact that there is little evidence to suggest they were heroes in any traditional sense of the word. And naturally, the embellished legacies of these men have added to the fame and lore of the town they called home. Instead of being a frontier boomtown that sought to add a sense of East Coast sophistication and entertainment that they could call "as good as" San Francisco, Tombstone has become an emblem of the frontier. Over 130 years after Tombstone peaked as a town, people associate it with gunfights, drunken cowboys, rugged vigilantes full of swagger, and the backdrop for the classic cops vs. robbers narrative. Tombstone is celebrated as the ultimate town of the Wild West, which itself continues to be widely celebrated for its lawlessness and viewed as uniquely American.

Today, Tombstone bills itself as the "Town Too Tough to Die." Less than 2,000 people call it home, and its only industry is tourism. Of course, the town is too tough to die because people continue to be fascinated by what Tombstone was well over a century ago, and everything represented by the historic Tombstone and people's imaginations of what it was like.

Bibliography

Agnew, Jeremy. *Entertainment in the Old West.* Jefferson, NC: McFarland & Company. 2011

Faulk, Odie B. *Tombstone: Myth and Reality.* New York: Oxford University Press. 1972.

Monahan, Sherry. *Tombstone's Treasure: Silver Mines and Golden Saloons.* Albuquerque, NM: University of New Mexico Press. 2007.

Smith, Richard Norton. *The Colonel: The Life and Legend of Robert R. McCormick, 1880 – 1885.* Evanston, IL: Northwestern University Press. 1997.

Deadwood

Chapter 1: The Birth of Deadwood

Before Deadwood became an iconic town of the western frontier, the area surrounding the Black Hills of southwestern South Dakota and eastern Wyoming was the land of the Lakota Sioux. The Lakota had claimed the land after they defeated the Cheyenne in 1776, and they called the mountains *Pahá Sápa*, or Black Hills, because the forest was so densely populated with trees that from a distance, the land appeared to be black. The Black Hills were so important to the Lakota that they considered it holy land and even incorporated it into their creation story. According to their legends, the first human reached the surface of the earth through a cave traditionally believed to be Wind Cave in the Black Hills.

In 1868, the United States government and the Lakota Sioux signed the Treaty of Laramie, which brought an end to Red Cloud's War in north-central Wyoming and removed the rival Ponca Indians from Lakota territory. The treaty stipulated that the Black Hills were to belong to the Lakota Sioux forever, "for the absolute and undisturbed use and occupancy of the Sioux." Whites could not enter the territory without the express permission of the Lakota, which was essential because the Black Hills were considered sacred to the natives. In addition, the Treaty of Fort Laramie dictated that the U.S. Army would abandon forts along the region.

It took less than a decade for things to change, as a result of the discovery of gold. The first rumors of gold in the region began to surface in 1834, long before the Laramie treaty was signed. A Jesuit missionary said he saw gold in the mountains, but when prospectors rushed in, the natives attacked them. Another group of white miners was chased out of the region in 1852. The Lakota Sioux knew there was gold on their land, but they didn't fully understand the value it held in white society.

Without promise of government help, private citizens took matters upon themselves. Charles

Collins, an Irishman from Sioux City, Iowa, led the campaign to open up the Black Hills to prospectors. Collins was an abolitionist who claimed to have been run out of Missouri for his anti-slavery views. He was also a newspaperman who saw an opportunity for Sioux City to flourish as miners passed through town on their way to the Dakota Territory. Energetic and known as something of a jokester, Collins' own path through the U.S. can be traced through the directories he published. These publications show Collins making his way through Colorado, Nevada, Kansas, and then Omaha, Nebraska.

By 1870, Collins had made his way across the Missouri River from Omaha to Sioux City. The town's riverfront location, and the fact that three railroads passed through, helped Sioux City grow to a population of 6,000 by the time Collins had arrived. Meat and wheat were exported from Sioux City, and it was an important wholesale and retail center, not to mention a center of Native American trade. The U.S. government contracted with Sioux City businessmen to provide the Sioux in the region with corn and pork, which was shipped up the Missouri River on steamboats to Indian agencies.

With the foundation already in place for Sioux City, Collins believed that opening up the Black Hills for mining would bring untold riches to the community, as well as force the Sioux to move out. He organized the Black Hills Mining and Exploring Association of Sioux City on February 27, 1872. With Collins as president of the organization and *Sioux City Journal* editor Dan Scott acting as vice-president, they launched an aggressive promotional campaign in the city newspapers. Thomas H. Russell, a prospector hired by the organization to develop an expedition, traveled up and down the Missouri River to speak to the townspeople and lecture about the opportunity just waiting for them all in the Black Hills. Soon, it seemed that all anyone wanted to talk about was gold mining.

White prospectors did not wait for the government to act and began to invade the Black Hills, despite warnings from the government that doing so could start a war with the Lakota Sioux. An anonymous letter to the *Sioux City Journal* warned that the death and destruction to the white people and the Native Americans was not worth all of the gold in the Black Hills. In a similar vein, U.S. Indian Agent H.D. Risley insisted that the Laramie treaty be enforced if the government was to maintain a positive relationship with the Lakota Sioux. On April 6, 1872, Department of Dakota commander General Winfield Scott Hancock, one of the Union's heroes at the Battle of Gettysburg almost a decade earlier, warned that anyone organizing or taking part in expeditions to the Black Hills was breaking federal law. Hancock said that the area would be protected by any means necessary, including the use of military force.

Winfield Scott Hancock

It would ultimately be the government itself that helped open the floodgate of miners into the Black Hills. General George Armstrong Custer was sent into the area in 1874 to select a location for a new military fort, as well to assess the land's gold resources. In August, New York newspapers printed headlines telling of the riches that Custer had found. By that fall, as many Americans were looking for a fresh start following the economic crisis of 1873, the gold rush was on. Within a year, over 15,000 miners had descended on the Black Hills. Lakota people, hunting within the confines of the territory promised to them by the Fort Laramie Treaty of 1868, began encountering white settlers and attacked them. Initially, when Americans demanded protection by the U.S. Army, the Army kept complying with the treaty and ejected the white interlopers.

Custer

The removal of white miners had the effect of increasing political pressure on the government to open the Black Hills to mining, logging, and settlement, and it was not only the prospectors who had an interest in seeing the region be mined for gold. The Gold Rush of 1849, which resulted in thousands of people flocking to California with visions of striking it rich, proved that there was money to be made outside of the gold mines too. Newspaper publishers, merchants, saloon keepers, and anyone else who stood to profit from the miners believed that the Lakota and the federal government were standing in the way of their right to make a living. To many, the solution seemed simple enough: buy the land back from the Lakota Sioux.

In May of 1875, several Lakota leaders traveled to Washington D.C. in the hope of convincing President Ulysses S. Grant to honor the treaty conditions. The government offered to buy the land for $6 million, but Sitting Bull, the Lakota tribal chief, declined the offer. To the Lakota Sioux, there could be no price tag on land that they considered holy. They would not consider selling the land, just as Catholics would never consider selling Vatican City.

Late in the fall of the same year, President Grant met with Major General Philip Sheridan and Brigadier General George Crook, and the three agreed to end the policy of ejecting miners and settlers. The President and the generals decided to notify Native American bands not already residing in the area that they had until January 31, 1876, to surrender to authorities and settle on reservations. Among these bands were those led by Sioux leaders Crazy Horse and Sitting Bull. The concept of ultimatums was foreign to Native Americans, and many bands were so far from existing reservations that they would be hard pressed to make it onto reservations before the deadline had passed even if they wanted to.

Sitting Bull

After the January 31, 1876 deadline came and went, the U.S. Army sent two columns of troops under Generals George Crook and Alfred Terry and a third column commanded by Colonel John Gibbon into the region in March of 1876. Over the next few months, the Army would battle the Lakota Sioux, who fought to hold onto the Black Hills. Despite the infamous defeat of Custer and the 7th Cavalry at the Battle of Big Horn on June 15, 1876, most of the Native Americans eventually surrendered or fled to Canada.

Within a matter of weeks during the summer of 1876, the town known as Deadwood would begin to take shape.

Chapter 2: Wild Bill, Calamity Jane, and the Summer of 1876

Deadwood had already been named in 1875, when a miner found gold in a narrow canyon lined with dead trees and called it Deadwood Gulch. That name stuck with the people that gave the town its shape and, in many ways, its character as they began to arrive in the summer of 1876. It was a turbulent summer for Deadwood. Native Americans were on the attack in the outlying communities, and even though the residents of Deadwood were armed enough to protect themselves, local newspapers were filled with stories of the often grisly battles between natives and whites. One such incident occurred in August, when the head of a murdered Native American was paraded through the streets of Deadwood. The head was given to a local doctor, who weighed it and determined that it was just 44 ounces, supposedly an indication that the dead man was not intelligent.

Even by 1874, Colorado Charlie Utter believed the Deadwood gold rush would be a "lallapaloozer." An experienced trapper and prospector, Utter was known as a "dandy." He made up for his short 5'6 stature with his appearance. His long blonde hair was always combed, as was his mustache. His fringed buckskins were made by hand, and he wore the finest linen shirts that he could afford. He completed his outfit with a large silver belt buckle, moccasins instead of boots, and pearl-handled revolvers. Utter was known to be extremely neat.

In the spring of 1876, Utter, his wife, and his brother, organized a wagon train. By the time the Utter party arrived, more than 100 people were in his contingent, including his old friend, Wild Bill Hickok. Utter was there to mine for gold, but when he did not make his fortune in the hills, he came up with other ways to make a living. He established a freight service and a mail service that delivered mail between Fort Laramie, Wyoming and Deadwood. The charge was 25 cents a letter with a delivery time of 48 hours. At one point, Utter's mail service delivered 5,000 letters per trip. Utter also opened a dance hall in nearby Lead in 1879, called the "Lower Dance Hall" or the "New Gem" (after Swearengen's Gem Theater). However, it was not nearly as successful as the real Gem, and Utter was fined $50 by the local court for running an establishment determined to be a public nuisance and for disturbing the peace. When he lost nearly all that he owned in the fire of September 1879, Utter left Deadwood. Some of his friends say that he spent his final years as an Indian doctor in Panama.

Though he was one of the most legendary gunmen of the West, Wild Bill Hickok was on the verge of blindness due to trachoma in 1876, and his gunfighting days were over by the time he first met Calamity Jane early that year. Jane was still a camp follower in February 1876 when she became part of an expedition against the Lakota-Sioux that was led by General George Crook in Laramie, Wyoming. While other stories about her scouting have been disputed, it is known that during this one Jane swam the Platte River and rode hard 90 miles to deliver dispatches, working at such a frenzied pace that she eventually fell ill and had to spend weeks recuperating. Her autobiographical statement also claimed, "During the month of June I acted as a pony express rider carrying the U.S. mail between Deadwood and Custer, a distance of fifty miles, over one of the roughest trails in the Black Hills country. As many of the riders before me had been held up and robbed of their packages, mail and money that they carried, for that was the only means of getting mail and money between these points. It was considered the most dangerous route in the Hills, but as my reputation as a rider and quick shot was well known, I was molested very little, for the toll gatherers looked on me as being a good fellow, and they knew that I never missed my mark. I made the round trip every two days which was considered pretty good riding in that country."

Wild Bill

Hickok, meanwhile, had recently married the former circus performer Agnes Lake, but he left his new bride in Cincinnati while he took a train back to Laramie in late spring in 1876. His plan was to join the gold rush headed for the Black Hills, and in June he got ready to leave Laramie to join his friend, Charlie Utter, on a wagon train that was leaving for South Dakota.

At the time, getting to the Black Hills was not easy. Bugs referred to as "sand gnats" continually buzzed around travelers, not to mention the problems that the deep gulches along the trail and the cold drizzling rain caused. The trip presented additional challenges because just as Utter and Hickok reached Fort Laramie, news came down from the Black Hills that Custer had been killed in Montana at the Battle of Little Big Horn. Attacks were not uncommon as the Lakota-Sioux attempted to protect their land from invasion by prospectors.

Due to the heightened awareness of trouble with Indians, the military suggested to Utter and Hickok that they join a larger group also going toward the Black Hills, which would provide them some additional protection against a possible attack. An officer also asked Hickok and Utter if they would take the wild woman that they had in the post guardhouse. As was typical for 20 year-old Jane, she had shown up at the fort right around payday and went on a drinking binge with some of the soldiers. As Hickok and Utter were discussing their plans to join the 30-wagon group looking for gold, she was sleeping off the effects of the alcohol, still partly drunk and partially naked. For whatever reason, the group agreed to take Jane along. The army provided her with military underwear and the wagon train, with no other clothing available for a woman, gave her a buckskin suit. Photographs of her in this suit perpetuated the idea that she dressed in men's clothing, although in this instance it was because she had no other choice.

Calamity Jane in her buckskin

Jane was not the only camp follower with the group. In fact, she was one of about a dozen women who were for all intents and purposes ladies of the evening, including well-known ladies like Madam Moustache and Dirty Em. Jane was mostly the primary companion to Steve Utter on the two-week trip, and occasionally she was with Charlie Utter, but by all accounts there was no romance of any type between her and Wild Bill. This was the first time he had ever seen her, and for the most part he merely tolerated her presence, although he appreciated that she helped out the wagon train by cooking meals. She proved to be a valuable mule-team driver, helping get the team over some rough spots, and she was indeed a good shot too. In the evening, when the men gathered around the fire to drink and tell stories, she was at home in that environment just as much as they were.

Many of the men found her tales, which were spiced up with cuss words not typically heard coming from a lady's mouth, quite entertaining. But Hickok was not one of those men. He was quiet most of the trip and had little to do with Jane, other than when she came around to get her tin cup filled from the keg of whiskey that he bought for the trip. When she needed a refill, she needed to see him, and at one point he told her to slow down and save some for the rest of the men. When the group reached Custer City, the southern region of the Black Hills, the few residents that had remained after finding out about the gold in nearby Deadwood thought little of Hickok. A newspaper reported that he looked like a bum, and the women he was with, including Jane, were not much better.

The group arrived in Deadwood around July 12 and made quite a spectacle of their arrival as they paraded down Main Street dressed in buckskin suits, but it was the arrival of Calamity Jane that a July 15 edition of the *Black Hills Pioneer* was most excited to report, with a headline blaring, "Calamity Jane has arrived!". No other members of her traveling party were mentioned by name at all, although this was not her first trip to Deadwood either. In 1875, she had accompanied the Walter Jenney expedition there, apparently snuck into the group by one of the soldiers. Few women could be found in mining towns, so when a woman arrived in a town like Deadwood, it was news, especially a woman like Calamity Jane.

Once she was there, Jane immediately became a popular dance hall girl, despite her rather masculine appearance. She became part of the hurdy-gurdy houses, where young ladies served as dance partners for the male patrons. There was no charge for the dancing, but following the dance it was expected that the men take their dance partners to the bar to buy drinks. The ladies and the proprietor of the dance house shared in the profits from the drinks. One prospector recalled seeing Jane wearing a fancy Stetson hat and a purple handkerchief as she danced with nearly everyone in the saloon, and then proceeded to the bar after every dance. It was also not an uncommon sight for Jane to dance with the women, just as the men did.

While it was not an automatic assumption that the dance hall girls were also prostitutes, it was not unheard of for some of the women to make extra money this way. The notorious proprietor Al Swearengen opened the "Gem Theater", a dance hall, in May 1876, and Jane was one of only three available dancers. In fact, the available pool of women for the dance hall was so slim that a young man who dressed as a woman was one of the dancers for a while. A bartender named Sam Young said that Jane once agreed to go to Sidney, Nebraska to round up more women for the Gem. After exaggerating the details about the money that could be made in Deadwood, Jane returned to town with 10 young girls ready to work for Swearengen.

The Gem Theater circa 1878. It's believed the man in the buggy on the left is Swearengen himself.

Jane did not camp out on the edge of town with Hickok and his fellow prospectors when they arrived in the summer of 1876, but she did return often for food, and the men later loaned her money so she could buy something to wear other than her buckskin suit. She pleaded her case, saying that she could hardly compete with the other women if she was not dressed properly, so Wild Bill kicked in $20 with the special request that she "wash behind her ears." After she earned some money from her exploits in the saloons and dance halls, she returned to the camp wearing a dress and stockings, from which she produced a roll of cash. She said business had been good and paid some of the men back, but Hickok refused to take any of the money, remarking, "At least she looks like a woman now."

Much of Calamity Jane's reputation ultimately came from her time in Deadwood. In one memorable scene, another member of Wild Bill's party, a woman named "Tid Bit," had agreed to spend time with a man called Laughing Sam. He paid her in gold dust, which ended up being a combination of sand and brass filings. Upon hearing of this, Jane borrowed Charley's two ivory-handled six-shooters and went to the saloon where she knew she would find Laughing Sam running a game of faro. Guns in hand, Jane burst into the saloon and proceeded to cuss out Laughing Sam until he agreed to give Tid Bit two $20 gold pieces.

Meanwhile, few if any members of Hickok's group recalled him actually prospecting for gold. However, on at least one occasion he did some target shooting in the woods one morning and still had enough skill to impress a reporter with his ability to shoot a tomato can out of the air. Though people have long believed Calamity Jane and Wild Bill were lovers, due to the fact Jane falsely claimed they were common law man and wife, the reporter, Leander Richardson from *The Springfield Republican* in Massachusetts, confirmed that Calamity Jane was enamored with Charlie Utter, called Colorado Charlie, not Hickok. Like Hickok, Charlie was a snappy dresser, and he fascinated the locals with his morning ritual of taking a bath, a completely unique habit back then. Utter was also as neat with his surroundings as he was with his appearance and kept a very tidy tent. One night after a drunken binge, Hickok went into Charlie's tent and fell asleep on his bed, which was made with fine linens and a blanket. When Charlie found him, he dragged Hickok out by his feet and threw him on the ground.

Although the legend of Deadwood has long prospered due to its association with Wild Bill Hickok, he was a shell of himself by the summer of 1876. At this point in his life, Hickok was most likely an alcoholic. Before he would even begin his day in earnest, the people in Deadwood would see him with his hair tied back into a knot, gun shoved into his belt, running toward the saloon to get a stash of liquor to bring back to his tent to help him get dressed and complete his morning routine. He was also addicted to poker, but some suggested that he was out of his league with the professional players in Deadwood.

Fittingly, the death of Wild Bill Hickok is shrouded in legend and mystery, and it's still not completely clear why he was shot by Broken Nose Jack McCall. It is believed that in a poker game on or around August 1, 1876, Hickok took all of the 24 year-old McCall's money. Allegedly, Hickok gave McCall a bit of his money back so that he could eat, but not before scolding McCall for betting more money than he had to lose. This was said to have enraged the young man.

McCall

Hickok was in Deadwood on August 2, 1876 to take part in a friendly card game at Saloon No. 10. To show how far Hickok's stock had fallen by the time he got to Deadwood, he found himself sitting with his back to the door, a table position he would never allow himself to take in the old days. Wild Bill had a habit of sitting with his back to a wall so he could see anyone and everyone coming toward him, a habit he had developed when he was making enemies as a marshal. This time, Wild Bill twice asked Charles Rich to change chairs with him, but he was ignored. A decade earlier, Hickok would only have had to direct a man to move, and he would have done so out of fear and/or respect.

The location of Saloon No. 10 in Deadwood

It's possible that Hickok wouldn't have stood a chance even with his back to the wall. As the game progressed, nobody paid any attention to Jack McCall, an indication that nobody had any reason to suspect he had a score to settle. As the table was playing 5 card draw, McCall approached Hickok from behind, shouted "Take that!" and fired a shot into the back of Hickok's head, killing him instantly. The shot was from such close range that the bullet exited Hickok's cheek and struck one of the other players, Captain Massie, in the wrist. As Hickok's lifeless body slumped onto the table, his cards fell from his hand, revealing two pair, black Aces and black 8s. Though a full house of Jacks over 10s used to be known back then as the Dead Man's Hand, Hickok's legendary death and hand eclipsed it, and Aces and 8s have been known as Dead

Man's Hand since Wild Bill's legend took off.

Charlie Utter would claim the body and filed a notice of his death in the *Black Hills Pioneer*: "Died in Deadwood, Black Hills, August 2, 1876, from the effects of a pistol shot, J. B. Hickock (Wild Bill) formerly of Cheyenne, Wyoming. Funeral services will be held at Charlie Utter's Camp, on Thursday afternoon, August 3, 1876, at 3 o'clock P. M. All are respectfully invited to attend."

In the aftermath of Wild Bill's death, Jane made one of her wilder claims:

"My friend, Wild Bill, remained in Deadwood during the summer with the exception of occasional visits to the camps. On the 2nd of August, while setting at a gambling table in the Bell Union saloon, in Deadwood, he was shot in the back of the head by the notorious Jack McCall, a desperado. I was in Deadwood at the time and on hearing of the killing made my way at once to the scene of the shooting and found that my friend had been killed by McCall. I at once started to look for the assassin and found him at Shurdy's butcher shop and grabbed a meat cleaver and made him throw up his hands; through the excitement on hearing of Bill's death, having left my weapons on the post of my bed. He was then taken to a log cabin and locked up, well secured as every one thought, but he got away and was afterwards caught at Fagan's ranch on Horse Creek, on the old Cheyenne road and was then taken to Yankton, Dak., where he was tried, sentenced and hung."

In reality, Jane had nothing to do with catching McCall. After stunningly shooting Hickok, McCall backed out of the saloon with his gun raised and made his way to his horse, but the cinch was loose and McCall fell to the ground. He ran for cover in the butcher shop but was discovered by a group of locals. McCall claimed that he shot Hickok in revenge for the death of his own brother in Kansas, but there is no evidence that he had a brother. Some say his feelings were bruised over the remarks Hickok made to him about betting over his head. Whatever the reason, an impromptu trial was held the next day among the local miners in the town. Even though there was no official law enforcement in Deadwood, the citizens tried to maintain some form of order with familiar mechanisms, such as jury trials. Despite overwhelming evidence that McCall killed Hickok in cold blood, he pleaded his case, saying that he was exacting revenge for his brother's death and that Hickok claimed that he would kill him too. Incredibly, McCall was declared innocent and set free, and he promptly left town, no doubt wary of retribution from Hickok's friends. In response to the verdict, the *Black Hills Pioneer* editorialized, "Should it ever be our misfortune to kill a man ... we would simply ask that our trial may take place in some of the mining camps of these hills."

The day after the trial, Charlie Utter arranged for Hickok's funeral. Wild Bill was laid out in a beautiful coffin in a teepee, where his friends and the people of Deadwood congregated to pay their last respects to one of the West's most famous icons. The grave marker read, "Wild Bill, J.

B. Hickock killed by the assassin Jack McCall in Deadwood, Black Hills, August 2, 1876. Pard, we will meet again in the happy hunting ground to part no more. Good bye, Colorado Charlie, C. H. Utter."

Steve and Charlie Utter at Wild Bill's grave

McCall refused to simply consider himself lucky to get away with murder. When he made it to Wyoming, he continued to talk about his one claim to fame and bragged about the killing of Wild Bill Hickok. When officials in Wyoming heard about it, they did not accept the verdict from the citizen court in Deadwood. McCall was formally charged and extradited to Yankton, South Dakota. Since Deadwood was not a legal jurisdiction, it was claimed that trying him would not be double jeopardy. Thus McCall stood trial again, and this time he was found guilty. McCall was hanged for the murder of Hickok on March 1, 1877. As the noose was being placed around his neck, McCall's reported last words were "draw it tighter, Marshal."

A reporter in town who claimed to talk to McCall filed a report (almost certainly wrongly) claiming, "As I write the closing lines of this brief sketch, word reaches me that the slayer of Wild Bill has been rearrested by the United State authorities, and after trial has been sentenced to death for willful murder. He is now at Yankton, D.T. awaiting execution. At the trial it was proved that the murderer was hired to do his work by gamblers who feared the time when better citizens should appoint Bill the champion of law and order – a post which he formerly sustained in Kansas border life, with credit to his manhood and his courage."

By 1902, Jane's exaggeration about her involvement with Hickok had progressed to marriage. Certainly her uncontrollable grief after Hickok's death, while sincere, contributed to the belief that she and Hickok had an intimate relationship, if not a marriage. Some say that she granted Hickok a divorce so he could marry Agnes Lake. However, in a 1902 interview she said that

Hickok was her fiancé and that they were due to be married days after he was shot. Claiming that law enforcement was doing nothing to locate Hickok's killer, she said she went to Yankton to bring the case against McCall to the grand jury and see that he was extradited and hanged for the murder. In reality, she was never married to Hickok, nor did she have anything to do with McCall's extradition to South Dakota.

Nevertheless, legend had it that when she died, her last words were to request that she be buried next to her husband Wild Bill, and people continued to run with it. In 1941, rumors of a relationship between Hickok and Calamity Jane persisted with the appearance of a woman saying that she was Jean Hickok McCormick. On May 6, McCormick went on the nationally broadcast CBS radio show "We the People" and said that she was the daughter of Wild Bill Hickok and Calamity Jane. She said she could prove it with a diary and letters written by Calamity Jane herself. Supposedly, this marriage occurred in Kansas in 1871 after Jane warned Hickok about a band of desperadoes headed his way, and then tended to his wounds after the battle. The documents claimed that a Reverend Warren married Jane and Hickok on the Kansas prairie, witnessed by several other men. The good reverend reportedly used a page from his Bible to scrawl out a marriage certificate. CBS Radio believed her and invited her to do a nationally broadcast interview. Apparently, the Billings Office of Public Welfare believed her and gave her the old age assistance that she requested.

McCormick went on to say that Hickok did not want his marriage to Calamity Jane to become public knowledge because he did not want either his wife or daughter to be in harm's way and used against him by outlaws. Therefore, he kept both his marriage and the birth of his daughter, which McCormick said occurred in a secluded cabin in Montana, a secret. Hickok was somehow able to hire an Indian to find the cabin and help Jane tend to her newborn child. The family never lived together and according to McCormick, it was when Hickok and Jane reunited in Deadwood that she granted Hickok his divorce so that he could marry Agnes Lake.

As for McCormick, she said that her mother gave her up for adoption and went to live with James O'Neill, a Liverpool sea captain for the Cunard Line who was living in Richmond, Virginia. McCormick claims that Jane visited her twice, although she never revealed her true identity. The second of these meetings allegedly occurred when Calamity Jane was traveling with Buffalo Bill Cody's Wild West Show in Richmond. McCormick said that after that show, she traveled with her mother when the tour moved on to England. McCormick's story was enough to convince the Billings, Montana public welfare office, which granted her request for old age assistance.

McCormick may have shared Calamity Jane's propensity for tall stories, but she didn't inherit it. Calamity Jane and Wild Bill were never married, and they never had a daughter. Put simply, none of McCormick's story was true. It was a well-established fact in the 19th century that Jane was illiterate and thus would have been incapable of writing the letters and the diary that

McCormick produced, which were filled with flowing prose and proper grammar. There was no such person as Captain James O'Neill, and Calamity Jane, while she did know Bill Cody, was never part of his show. McCormick omits from her story that Calamity Jane was a known alcoholic, later married a man named Bill Steers and had a daughter named Jessie. Despite this, McCormick was buried in a Billings grave with a tombstone reading that she was the daughter of Wild Bill Hickok and Calamity Jane. Unfortunately, many people believed the fraudulent story, which continues to complicate the truth about Calamity Jane.

When Calamity Jane died in 1903, she was ultimately buried alongside Wild Bill, though the reasons for it have long been debated. It was said that Calamity Jane visited Hickok's grave often, and that he had been reinterred and moved at her request. Wild Bill was initially laid to rest in Ingleside Cemetery in Deadwood, but after the cemetery filled up, Wild Bill was moved to Mount Moriah Cemetery. Part of the legend of Calamity Jane is that she supposedly asked to be buried next to Hickok as her dying request, while others say that because Wild Bill had no use for her in life, she was buried next to him for all eternity as a joke. However, the most likely explanation is that town officials in Deadwood decided to bury Calamity Jane next to Wild Bill Hickok to boost tourism. Wild Bill's wife, Agnes, who never saw Hickok again after he left Cincinnati to join the gold rush to the Black Hills, was buried next to her first husband instead of Hickok when she died in 1907.

Chapter 3: Deadwood Takes Shape

In September 1876, the only official regulatory body in the mining camp, the Board of Health, called for Deadwood Gulch and the several small nearby camps to be incorporated into one town. Almost overnight, Deadwood attracted about 3,000 residents and nearly 200 businesses. Mail service arrived for the first time on September 25, and the telegraph followed in December. For a dollar a night, travelers could stay at the Grand Central, the first hotel in Deadwood. Owner Charles Wagner provided a primitive wooden bunk or perhaps a space on the floor with a blanket depending on the crowd. Miners often cooked their own food and subsisted on a diet of biscuits and beans until restaurants opened. At 18 cents a pound, beans were very economical, especially compared to the $60 a 100-pound bag of flour cost in the first winter.

With no regulatory body there and people flooding in left and right, the earliest days of Deadwood saw the establishment of an entirely lawless mining camp; the miners and the residents tended to take matters into their own hands if a crime was committed. Deadwood fell in the middle of a legal loophole because the boomtown was outside of U.S. jurisdiction. Maintaining law and order in Deadwood was a challenge because Deadwood was not even supposed to exist. Further complicating matters was the issue that Deadwood was still technically on Sioux land, since the fighting had not technically resolved the issue of ownership between the U.S. and the Native Americans. Laws could not be passed, let alone enforced, on land that the U.S. did not possess. This made for a chaotic environment that relied on sporadic self-policing to try and keep some semblance of order, often with minimal success.

Although "the coward McCall" was put before an impromptu jury after shooting Hickok and was (theoretically) given due process, the system and result led to the belief that an official law enforcement system was needed in Deadwood. And according to legend, one of the men most suited to enforce the law was in Deadwood at the time. Wyatt Earp, the West's most legendary lawmen, is believed to have been in Deadwood for a brief spell during the time, but he was there to mine for gold like just about everyone else. Bat Masterson had told Earp that there was not much available for the small-time prospector, but Earp headed to Deadwood anyway to see if he might get lucky. He quickly discovered that Masterson had been right, so his stay in Deadwood was brief. Legend has it that Seth Bullock advised Earp that if he was thinking of becoming the sheriff in Deadwood that he could move on because his services were not needed. Most people in Deadwood believed that Bullock was the most logical choice to be the town's first sheriff anyway.

Wyatt Earp

Seth Bullock

    Although the popular HBO series on Deadwood depicted a budding friendship between Bullock and Hickok, Bullock actually arrived in Deadwood the day before Hickok's murder. He and his friend and business partner, Sol Star, knew a good opportunity when they saw one. They decided that the hardware store they owned in Helena, Montana would be a good fit in the mining community of Deadwood. As soon as they rolled into town in their ox-driven wagon, they began auctioning off the contents, which included frying pans, dutch ovens, chamber pots, and various mining equipment. Not long after that, Bullock and Star purchased a corner lot on Main Street. A year later, the corner was the site of their new hardware store and warehouse. Today it is the location of the Bullock Hotel, which some say is haunted by the ghost of Seth Bullock himself.

A picture of the hardware store

In addition to owning a hardware store, Bullock and Sol Star also partnered with Harrison Franklin and opened the first grain mill in Deadwood. Star was part of the town council soon after he arrived and was named the postmaster in 1877. Unfortunately for Star, he was wrongly accused of stealing $2,000 from a letter mailed to Deadwood and was forced to resign after three years. Star worked hard to restore his reputation, and he would be elected mayor in 1884. He was mayor of Deadwood for 14 years, and after South Dakota became a state in 1889, Star served for the state legislature.

Sol Star

    Within about a month of his arrival, Bullock was the de facto sheriff, a position made official by territorial governor John Pennington in 1877, after Lawrence County was formed. In 1878, Bullock was made U.S. deputy marshal. It was not Bullock's first job as sheriff, which would explain why he had the gall to confront Wyatt Earp if that confrontation actually took place. Bullock had previously been the sheriff of Lewis and Clark County in Montana, and he had the look of a frontier sheriff. With his tall and rugged stature, he could often fix a man with a steely glare alone if needed, and his grandson claimed Seth could "outstare a mad cobra or a rogue elephant." The claims had to have been somewhat true, since Bullock never killed a man during his time as a lawman in South Dakota.

    Once he was appointed sheriff, Bullock surrounded himself with deputies that he trusted to take on the rough and tumble elements in town, and by the end of 1876, Bullock had managed to instill some sense of law and order. For the sheriff of Deadwood, upholding the law meant more than breaking up bar fights. Bullock was kept busy with settling mining claim disputes, fighting off Native American attacks, and tracking down horse thieves and stagecoach robbers. If there was a trial, Bullock was the one to preside over it. If there was a murder, he investigated it. If prisoners were locked up in the local jail or had to be extradited to another city or state, Bullock was responsible for overseeing them too. He also took on the responsibility of tending to his town's reputation and, as a result, kept a close watch on the other two big industries in Deadwood other than mining: gambling and prostitution.

    Bullock was also more than the sheriff and marshal. He founded the town's Board of Health, which agreed to build a facility for smallpox victims after a smallpox epidemic went through Deadwood in the summer of 1876. The health commission also established fire and sanitation codes, established the police and fire department, and created the first cemetery in Deadwood. Bullock's negotiations with the Fremont, Elkhorn and Missouri Valley Railroad helped bring train service to the region and made the Black Hills into one of the most active livestock shipping ports in the nation.

Bullock's wife, Martha, was also an important part of the new community, although she did not join him right away. Bullock knew that a mining camp was no place for his wife and infant daughter, so it was not until July 1878 that a stagecoach from Cheyenne arrived with Bullock's wife and daughter. Jane founded the Round Table Club, a ladies literary group that still exists in Deadwood today. In 1895, the Round Table Club helped establish the first town library. Jane was also very active in church activities and other community events.

Martha Bullock

Not much is known about Ethan Bennett Farnum before his arrival in Deadwood in the summer of 1876, other than the fact he came from Wisconsin and opened a general store soon after bringing his wife and three children to the mining camp. Farnum also invested in other properties in the region, including some on Main Street, as well as two of the area mines. In August, Deadwood held its first mayoral election, and of the 1,139 votes cast, Farnum won 672.

Being elected the mayor of a town that had dirt roads just a rainfall away from becoming a mud bog and whose complete lack of a sanitation system created a haven for rats was hardly a glamorous job. Some of Farnum's first tasks included creating a street cleaning system, the first fire department, and a facility for quarantining smallpox victims. Perhaps not surprisingly, the influx of a lot of people also brought diseases. The *Black Hills Daily Pioneer* reported on August 12, 1876 that a mild epidemic had broken out, and the "pest house" was opened a week later.

Farnum's position of mayor also came with the duties of justice of the peace and judge. When Fannie Garretson and Daniel Brown became the first couple to marry in Deadwood, Farnum officially married them. He also sent the town's first telegram – a message to the mayor of Cheyenne – and worked with the South Dakota territorial government to see that Deadwood was formally recognized as a town. When Farnum lost the next mayoral election, he left Deadwood for Chicago. Unfortunately, records about any other contributions he made to the establishment of Deadwood were lost in the fire that swept through town in 1879.

The first missionary to brave the tumultuous mining camp was Harry Weston "Preacher" Smith. Like the founder of the Methodist faith, John Wesley, Smith left his family behind and answered what he believed to be God's call to him by trying to bring Christianity to the lawless frontier. In May 1876, after having left his family in Kentucky, Smith held a church service in the small town of Custer City, believed to be the first Christian church service in the Black Hills.

After his second service the following week, Smith asked Captain C.V. Gardner if he could walk with his wagon train, which was headed for Deadwood. Gardner agreed, and he even refused to accept the $5 that Smith offered for allowing him to accompany his group. Three days later, Smith and the Gardner wagon train arrived. With no church, Gardner took to the streets to preach. Gardner later said that any stories about Smith going into the saloons to preach to the miners are fiction, because most of Deadwood was centered on Main Street and Smith had no trouble finding an audience right on the street every Sunday.

Main St., looking at the Gem Theater

Being a street preacher was no way to make a living though, and Smith took work where he could find it. He was also known to do a bit of prospecting in the hills. On August 20, 1876, after Smith finished his Sunday morning service near the corner of Main and Gold Streets, he wrote a note and stuck it on the door of his cabin. The note said that he had gone to Crook City to lead a service there, and "if God is willing," he would return at 3 p.m.

Smith's friends had warned him about walking through the woods alone. Native American attacks on the outskirts of Deadwood were not uncommon, as some of the Lakota Sioux still sought to avenge the loss of their land, even if the war with the U.S. was officially over. Just the previous day, a mail carrier named Charles "Red" Nolin was killed while delivering mail along the trail between Sidney, Nebraska and Deadwood. Nolin had stopped at Alkali Creek, where he met up with a wagon train that had been hauling hay. The freight men had urged Nolin to stay with them because they had heard war cries nearby. However, Nolin was in a hurry and wanted to finish his ride because he had told his mother in Nebraska that he would not do another mail run after this one. Nolin did not stay with the wagon train, and the men found his mutilated body laying amidst the scattered mail the following morning.

Smith said he was not worried and that the Bible was his protection. However, Smith's body was found about midway between Deadwood and Crook City later that day. He had been shot once through the chest. When Bullock wrote to Reverend J.S. Chadwick to inform him of Smith's death, he blamed it on the Native Americans. The killer was never found though, and some believed a white man who did not like Smith's preaching killed him. Certainly some people did not want to see Deadwood reformed from its lawless ways, since that would have been bad for the liquor, gambling, and prostitution businesses.

Chapter 4: The Fire of 1879

Just as Deadwood was making the transition from wild frontier town to a profitable commercial center of the Black Hills, disaster struck. On September 26, 1879, a fire started at Mrs. Ellsner's Empire Bakery and made its way to Jensen and Bliss's Hardware Store. Perhaps the initial fire could have been contained had it not been for the fact the hardware store housed eight kegs of blasting powder essential for mining operations. Once the fire hit the blasting powder, there was an explosion that shook all of Deadwood, and from there the fire spread up the hill and destroyed all of the homes along that narrow streets that overlooked Main Street.

Chaos ensued as the residents of Deadwood tried in vain to get up the hill to rescue their homes and possessions. In one quarter-mile area, nearly 300 buildings were destroyed and 2,000 people were left homeless. The total property loss was valued at $3 million, an impressive figure for a 19th century mining town just three years old. Unfortunately, most of the buildings were uninsured, and one of the destroyed buildings was the post office, which lost $3,000 worth of stamps but no mail.

Once the fire was brought under control, prominent citizens in the town held a meeting to plan the next steps. Looting was already underway, as was lot jumping, which consisted of someone deciding that a lot with a burned building was now fair game and available for the taking. Therefore, the first order of business was to call General Samuel Sturgis at Fort Meade and request troops to help combat criminal activity. Sturgis quickly responded with a company of cavalry, 10 wagons, and two ambulances, all for transporting residents of Deadwood to Fort Meade to receive food and shelter.

Seth Bullock ordered that all saloons be closed to help prevent any alcohol-fueled crime sprees, which left the streets of Deadwood unusually quiet, and a local citizen's committee organized to help Bullock patrol the streets and keep the peace. When order was restored, the citizens of Deadwood went about the task of trying to rebuild. Fortunately, once the bank vaults had cooled enough to open them, bankers discovered that the money inside them was not damaged, so there was funding available for the massive rebuilding project.

It was a community effort to get Deadwood functioning again. There were few, if any reports, of price gouging or other unscrupulous business tactics, and miners were able to scrape together enough gold dust from their equipment to resume prospecting. As new buildings were constructed, they were made of stone and brick rather than wood, a reflection of the Victorian Era. Even the West's most legendary frontier towns wanted to embrace the styles of the East. Within six months, Deadwood had taken on a new, more cosmopolitan appearance, but one loss that could not be recouped was the destruction of many of Deadwood's original records, leaving a gaping hole for modern researchers tracing the history of the famous frontier town.

Chapter 5: Al Swearengen and the Gem

The interior of the Gem. The man behind the counter with the mustache might be Swearengen.

"Al Swearengen gazed into the barrel of a revolver which was aimed at him last night. The hostile was disarmed by a bystander, and was put in his little bed." – The *Black Hills Pioneer*

Many times the stories that are written about the men and women of the West are largely mythical. In most cases, their exploits are made out to be more fantastic than they really were. But for Al Swearengen, a mostly forgotten individual whose name and reputation were brought roaring back to life in the HBO series about Deadwood, it may very well be the opposite. As the owner and operator of the Gem, which was a combination of a brothel, saloon, and entertainment venue, Swearengen was as brutal and ruthless as he has been made out to be, and perhaps even more so.

When the Civil War veteran arrived in Deadwood at about the same time as all of the other original entrepreneurs in the summer of 1876, he was not thinking about the gold mines. His plan was to "mine the miners." He knew that the men that searched for gold by day would have money in their pockets and a need for a place to spend it at night. Swearengen's first business in Deadwood was the Cricket Saloon, named for a coal mining camp in his native Iowa. The Cricket was only 8 feet wide but it was 60 feet long, making it resemble a long and narrow hallway.

Swearengen's plan for the Cricket was to lure miners into the establishment by offering alcohol and fights. He called them prizefights, even though nobody won any money. The draw was simply watching men beat each other to a pulp in a makeshift boxing ring at the back of the saloon. Three walls provided one barrier and a row of benches provided the other. If the action in the 5x5 ring was not enough, there were often fights among the spectators to spice up any dull moments. Given that the only way to see what was happening in the fights was to crowd up against the benches, those kinds of brawls broke out fairly regularly.

The first fight at the Cricket featured Johnny Marr and George Latimer. Both men were dressed in trousers, shirt, and socks. By the end of the 40th round, they had dispensed with the shirts. The referee, a local saloon owner named Billy Nuttall, declared the fight a draw after 52 rounds. The fight was front page news in Deadwood, and the next day, *The Black Hills Pioneer* gave it two full columns of coverage.

Swearengen made enough money at the Cricket that he was able to open the Gem Variety Theater on April 7, 1877. Located on the corner of Wall and Main, the Gem was far more upscale than the Cricket, and the *Black Hills Pioneer* boasted that it was as "neat and tastefully arranged as any place of its kind in the west." It was also much larger than the Cricket, standing two stories tall and measuring 30 feet x 100 feet with a 24-foot façade. As customers entered the Gem, there was a large bar with tables for seating. To the left was a large room that was used as a dance hall.

Swearengen's office and apartment were located above the dance hall, and also on the second floor was a balcony where a band was stationed, filling Main Street with the sound of music designed to lure customers into the Gem. Just inside the balcony, one could see directly down to the theater. Private boxes ringed the theater, and if needed, a curtain could be drawn in each box to keep prying eyes from witnessing what was happening inside.

Swearengen took great care in creating the theater. It featured a stage with custom designed drop curtains. The first manager of the Gem, J.M. Martin, painted the scenery panels. It was also important to Swearengen that the Gem have the best entertainment possible, so he did not hesitate to bring in acts from around the country. Sam Murdy from Cheyenne performed a comedy show on the Gem's opening night, and other entertainment included Walter Parkes, who was renowned as one of the best African-American comedians in the nation, Baby McDonald, a child singing and dancing sensation, and Baby McDonald's father, a skater and champion clog dancer. The Gem put on plays, and occasionally even an opera singer would perform.

However, entertainment was not the only moneymaker for the Gem. Swearengen's establishment was also a brothel. Prostitution was hardly unusual in the West; in fact, it was expected in mining towns and typically was not hidden. The women who worked for Swearengen, though, were often tricked into becoming prostitutes. He brought groups of women in from the East under the false pretense that they would be performers in his theater, paying only for one way trips. When they arrived, they discovered that he really expected them to be prostitutes. If they refused, Swearengen reminded them that he paid for their journey to Deadwood, and he would then demand either the money that they almost certainly didn't have to repay him, or he would demand the services he expected from them. With no money to return home and no other way to make money in Deadwood, they had little choice but to comply.

Many of the young women Swearengen employed were underage and did not speak English. They lived in small rooms on the second floor, and if they tried to escape, talk back, or do anything else that Swearengen did not like, they were beaten by Johnny Burns, who managed the girls, or by Swearengen himself. It was not unusual at all to see one of the Gem girls sporting bruises or cuts. Swearengen thought nothing of humiliating the women in his employ or getting them hooked on laudanum, an opiate that was legal at the time. In fact, Swearengen's wife, Alma, had a laudanum habit herself. The drug no doubt masked some of the pain from the life the young women were forced to lead, but even then it wasn't enough for all of them. On one occasion, one teenage prostitute was so despondent that she shot and killed herself in her room.

In the spring of 1878 Swearengen threw a masquerade ball at the Gem, and since most of the residents in Deadwood didn't have costumes, Swearengen imported them from other places. It took time to bring in all the costumes due to dangers along the roads, but by that June, the ball could be thrown. On June 1, the *Black Hills Pioneer* reported that the suits "have now arrived, and this evening at the Gem Theatre the boys and girls may expect to have a fine time. Suits may be obtained at the theatre."

These performances, and a casual lack of interest, tended to keep Swearengen out of the crosshairs of the people in town, but he found himself under arrest for battery later that summer. A miner named Tom Clark got drunk and rowdy, as many men in the Gem were apt to do, but apparently he was so abusive that Swearengen decided to throw him out. One can only imagine how bad Clark's behavior had to be to get kicked out of an establishment like the Gem, but by the time Clark was out the doors, his head and face were badly cut and bruised. Clark came back with a gun and threatened Swearengen, even demanding that Swearengen arm himself for a duel, but cooler heads ultimately prevailed thanks to the law, which detained Swearengen. Swearengen had to post a $250.00 bond to get out.

While Swearengen's ways were proof of the seedy and lawless elements in Deadwood, it's also believed that Swearengen got away with this behavior because he struck a deal with Seth Bullock. They supposedly agreed to divide Main Street into two sections. Swearengen got lower

Main Street, which became known as the "Badlands", and the law got upper Main Street. Bullock wasn't a corrupt lawman so much as he recognized the limits of his own power. Swearengen was one of the most powerful men in Deadwood, and there was no shortage of residents who frequented the Gem and simply accepted Swearengen's tactics and forms of entertainment as nothing to be alarmed about.

Even still, Swearengen began to feel pressure from the community when the *Black Hills Daily Times* published an article in September 1884 with the headline "Infamous: A Den of Prostitution under the Guise of a Dance Hall, Stock with Innocent and Unsuspecting Girls Engaged through Misrepresentation by its Bestial Proprietor." Two days earlier, a new group of 11 young girls arrived in Deadwood after responding to an advertisement in a Chicago newspaper. When the girls found out the true nature of their work, they refused but were locked in their rooms at the Gem. One of the girls managed to escape and reported Swearengen to local law enforcement, which freed three other girls.

The Gem was extremely profitable for Swearengen, often bringing in over $5,000 a night and sometimes even $10,000. Even when the original Gem burned down in September 1879, Swearengen had no trouble financing a new Gem, and his profit making resumed. He had his enemies, though. The local Methodist church called for the Gem's closure, and Swearengen was arrested on charges of assault more than once, including for abusing all three of his wives. Bullock even went so far as to close the Gem for 48 hours and allow it to be sold at an auction, but nobody dared to bid against Swearengen, so it remained in his possession.

By the mid-1880s, any pretense of the Gem being a respectable theater was gone. Neighbors frequently complained of the noise, law enforcement was called in on a regular basis to break up fights, and the Gem's side of Main Street were ubiquitously known as the Badlands. The Gem was gone for good after another fire broke out on December 19, 1899. There were certainly odd circumstances surrounding the fire. Witnesses said that the fire seemed to start in six different places at once, and when the fire alarm went off, it sounded outside of the Gem's ward. When the first firefighters responded, they mysteriously could not locate the nozzles for their hoses or their wrenches for the fire hydrants. The second and third fire companies had the same problem. Swearengen had actually had water pumps installed in the Gem after the first fire, but the men in the Gem could not fight the blaze themselves. Meanwhile, as the Gem burned to the ground, all other surrounding buildings were spared.

It would have come as a surprise to no one if the fire had been set intentionally. Swearengen realized this too and ultimately left town. One local newspaper bid the Gem and Swearengen good riddance by saying the business was the "ever-lasting shame of Deadwood." One newspaper account reported that "harrowing tales of iniquity, shame and wretchedness; of lives wrecked and fortunes sacrificed; of vice unhindered and esteem forfeited, have been related of the place, and it is known of a verity that they have not all been groundless."

The interior of the Gem in 1880

Not much is known about Swearengen after he left town, but some scholars believe trouble followed him. When he went to visit his twin brother Lemuel in Iowa, Lemuel was shot 5 times but not robbed in broad daylight in the street, and many people assumed he had been mistaken for his notorious brother Al. Al skipped town after the attack on Lemuel, but he died two months later in Denver, Colorado in November 1904. His body was found with a massive head wound near a streetcar track. It's unclear whether he died while drunkenly trying to jump onto a car or if someone had hit him in the head, but he had certainly made enough enemies that the latter is certainly possible.

Chapter 6: Entertainment in Deadwood

With money in their pockets and nowhere to go but Main Street to spend it, entertainment was an important part of Deadwood in its formative years. Gambling, especially card games such as poker and faro, were very popular, but it was the theater that provided much of Deadwood's earliest entertainment.

A town as rough around the edges as Deadwood in the late 19th century might seem like an unusual place for theater, but live performances were a popular form of entertainment. By the summer of 1876, Deadwood already had its first theater, and by the beginning of the 20th century, Deadwood had six theaters and opera houses. These places featured a variety of entertainment, including comedy, plays, singers, and the local favorite, burlesque.

Burlesque was a blend of comedy routines, especially ones that took a satirical look at the upper crust of Victorian society, with choreographed dance routines by female dance troupes. When burlesque first began, the performances were takes on famous stage plays, operas, and musicals, but as time went on, burlesque took on a more forbidden reputation as costumes became skimpier and the dialogue became more daring. The sexual innuendo of the earliest Hollywood films took a cue from burlesque, and unsurprisingly, the mostly male audiences of Deadwood approved of the content.

In addition to the Gem, there were two other main theaters in Deadwood. Actor and producer Jack Langrishe took his acting troupe to Deadwood in 1876, where he rented the McDaniels Theater. By day, the McDaniels Theater had been used for court proceedings, funeral services, dances, or as a reception hall for distinguished guests, but when Langrishe took over the building, he renamed it the Langrishe Theater and staged performances, sometimes in exchange for gold dust. While it was a small wooden building with only a canvas roof, it quickly became a place to be seen as much as it was a place to take in a show. It was also one of the few establishments in town at the time that a woman could frequent without having her morals questioned.

Langrishe

The first performance by Langrishe's acting company was on the evening of July 22, 1876. They followed that up with a performance of "Trodden Down, or Under Two Flags," a popular play written by the actor Harry Watkins. By all accounts, the Deadwood theatergoers considered the performance a great success. Langrishe's theater hosted a wide variety of performances, including a burlesque act inspired by the great Swedish opera singer of the day, Jenny Lind. Business was brisk for Langrishe, and customers paid as much as $25 a ticket for the best seats in the house. Many believed that the performances at the Langrishe Theater were on par with what could be found in New York City, and some of the shows produced there were also running in New York and London.

In 1879, Langrishe followed many of the miners who began to migrate toward Leadville, Colorado, where gold had been found. The final Deadwood performance by the Langrishe Company was on August 14, and the audience was treated to "Our American Cousin," a comedy by British playwright Tom Taylor. The play had also gained some notoriety for being the production that Abraham Lincoln was watching at Ford's Theater the night he was assassinated in April 1865. Johnny Rogers leased the Langrishe Theater after Jack Langrishe left, and the Metropolitan acting company performed there until the fire of 1879.

Tom Miller, who also owned several other nearby properties, owned the upscale Bella Union Theater. It was the nicest establishment in Deadwood when it opened in 1876; the Bella Union had three main grand entrances, 30-foot ceilings, and an opulent private reception room that was often used by the locals as a meeting room. In addition to the theater with 17 private boxes, the Bella Union also had a bar and a few gaming tables. More than stage performances were featured here. Locals could also see wrestling tournaments, boxing exhibitions, and even a trapeze act. Miller billed his theater as entertainment for "ladies and families."

However, the Bella Union was only open for two years. Miller went bankrupt in November 1878 and was forced to sell off the theater's scenic panels and fixtures. The first floor of the building became a grocery store, and the upper floor was called Mechanics Hall. Perkins and Company tried to revive Mechanics Hall as a theater in January 1879, but as miners began to drift away from Deadwood, the town was unable to support Mechanics Hall. With Langrishe's company gone, only Al Swearengen's Gem remained as an option for Deadwood's theatergoers.

The Bella Union after it was sold

Prostitution was an institution in Deadwood for nearly 100 years, and there was more to Deadwood's prostitution business than the Gem even in Deadwood's early days. Two madams calling themselves Dirty Em and Madam Mustachio were among the first to arrive in town in 1876 as part of Charlie Utter's wagon train. They knew the mining business well and had been previously located in mining camps in California and Nevada. When the ladies rolled into town, the Deadwood miners were so happy to see them that they cheered the very sight of them.

In the earliest weeks of Deadwood, it is estimated that as many as 90 percent of the women in town were prostitutes. If a woman was in Deadwood and did not have a husband to support her, she had little other choice than to turn to prostitution to make enough money to survive. Still, even for women who anticipated being prostitutes in Deadwood, it was a difficult life for most of the young women who found themselves working in brothels. Drug addiction was common, and for those who could no longer take the pain of what their lives had become, overdoses and suicide attempts were not uncommon. The town doctor, F.S. Howe, was known to bring a stomach pump on any late-night call to the Badlands because chances were a young woman had overdosed on laudanum or perhaps morphine. If men like Swearengen had not got them hooked on the drugs, it was Howe himself, who believed that keeping the girls "medicated" would reduce the number of calls he received.

Despite all of this, many of the prostitutes made good money because their services were in such demand. With men outnumbering women 200 to 1 in Deadwood, a man was willing to pay whatever the going rate was for some female companionship. It did not even matter that in the earliest days of Deadwood, brothels were simply tents until permanent structures could be built. The madams, who received 40 percent of the money that went to the working girls, stood to make the most profit, but alcohol was the biggest moneymaker. A patron to a brothel was expected to at least buy one drink for himself as well as one for the woman that would share his company. The money that the madams took was spent on room, board, and bouncers, who would remove a man who got too aggressive with his advances.

One of the most popular madams of the era was Madam Dora Dufran, an English immigrant who was just 15 years old when the gold rush hit Deadwood. She was known to be kind to her working girls and later turned her home into a charity hospital during the flu epidemic of 1918. Alabama native Mollie Johnson, who was called the Queen of Blondes in Deadwood because of the three blonde ladies in her employ, was also noted for her kindness. Despite the fact they were competitors, Johnson and Dufran got along well. Eventually, Johnson left the Deadwood area in 1883 due to lack of business.

Dora Dufran

Even when Deadwood's economy faltered, most of the brothels remained open. In fact, they remained open decades after Deadwood was established and long after miners no longer came. Richard Furze, a local prosecutor, tried to close down Deadwood's brothers in 1951. In his first attempt, he arrested prostitutes, but they would simply pay the fines and go back to work. When he tried another raid on the night of a major town event that was sure to attract many customers to the brothels, the madams hired an attorney from Rapid City to defend them. The case went to trial, and after a 10-minute deliberation the jury determined that the madams were not guilty. Furze finally caught on to the idea that the residents of Deadwood did not mind having brothels in town and gave up trying to close them.

William Carnahan, Furze's successor, tried to go after the brothels a few years later but got tripped up with some paperwork technicalities. The town wasted little time in voting him out of office when they got the chance. As far as the town was concerned, the brothels were welcome because they were discreet and the owners were generous when it came time to give to local charities. However, when the owner of Pam's Purple Door was implicated in organized crime activity and the murder of a judge in Texas in 1979, it was the beginning of the end of prostitution in Deadwood.

With the federal government now looking into Deadwood's prostitution, the world's oldest profession was finally shut down in 1980 when Judge Ed Brandenburg said that the town's last two brothels were a public nuisance. Many people wrote him letters and asked him to let the brothels stay open, but he was clear on the fact that even if he did have an appreciation for Deadwood's storied past, the law was clear on the matter of prostitution.

Chapter 7: Chinese Immigrants in Deadwood

Like many people who found their way to Deadwood, Chinese immigrants arrived in the Black Hills in search of gold in the 1880s. Many had just finished working on the railroad and headed to Cheyenne or Sidney, where they could take a stagecoach to Deadwood. One of the first Chinese men who arrived in search of gold was Fee Lee Wong, the cook for a small group of white prospectors. When the group arrived in Deadwood in 1876, claims were divided among the men in the group. One of the miners did not want Fee Lee to have a claim, but the rest of the party disagreed, so Fee Lee was given two claims. When gold was found next to Fee Lee's claim, some said that he sold his for $75,000, but with most of Deadwood's early records being destroyed in the fire, nobody knows for sure if the transaction really happened.

Fee Lee

Most of the Chinese population made a living away from the mines and could be found earning money other ways, but this was not because the Chinese in Deadwood did not want to work in the mines. The white men who felt threatened by their presence legally shut them out. If the Chinese were permitted to work the mines, it was usually in the worst mining ground and in areas that white men did not want to work, leaving them abandoned. Still, a few Chinese prospectors had success, and one Chinese miner discovered a $400 gold nugget in 1878. This was at a time when miners made between about $4 and $7 a day.

Overall, it was more diplomatic for the Chinese to open businesses to serve the miners, such as boarding houses, restaurants, and laundry facilities called "washee" houses. Laundries were a favorite because they were inexpensive to run. For less than $20, a Chinese entrepreneur could open a laundry facility in Deadwood. Wood could be taken from the forest, and the nearby creek provided a steady supply of water, free of charge. The Chinese grew to have a monopoly on laundry in Deadwood, because any white people who tried to provide competition were drummed out of business when the Chinese laundries cut their rates far below what the newcomers could match. When the competition left, the Chinese bumped their rates back up. A good businessman or woman could clear up to $10 a day in profit. Some also managed to make some money by saving the wash water and retrieving the gold dust that came off of the miners' dirty laundry.

There were also seven Chinese-owned restaurants in Deadwood in 1898, but they did not serve Chinese food. They learned quickly what the miners wanted to eat, which was mainly steak and potatoes. The proprietor of the Bodega Café liked to joke with his customers. Wong Kee would ask a miner what kind of pie he wanted and after the miner replied, Wong would laugh and say, "We have apple."

The census indicates the peak number of Chinese residents was 250, but locals say that the real number was twice that amount. This might have been because many Chinese did not trust the government and avoided giving the census taker any information. Whatever the real number, those that were there were created a vibrant community of their own. Deadwood's Chinatown had its own churches, boarding houses, bakeries, markets, gambling halls, and opium dens. If there was anything besides doing laundry that might lure a white miner to Chinatown, it was the opium den. The opium dens were legal until 1909, and just like saloons, they were regulated and paid yearly taxes.

The Chinese also recreated the temples and gardens of their homeland. Some converted to Christianity, but many attended the Joss House, or temple. Deadwood's Chinatown even had its own mayor, fire department, and police department. There was no law in the Dakota Territory against immigrants owning property, so many of the Chinese owned the buildings in which they opened businesses. For the most part, they had to create their own community because they were tolerated more than welcomed in Deadwood. Many of the white men found the Chinese culture a bit too mysterious for their liking, and the Chinese were not allowed to walk on Main Street at night, so they were forced 12 feet underground. A lengthy network of tunnels that were created when the streets of Deadwood were raised and the wooden sidewalks were paved served as the primary walkway for Chinese residents.

An exception to that rule was Fee Lee Wong, who took his mining profits and invested them in the Wing Tsue Emporium on Main Street. The store sold Chinese groceries, silks, traditional medicines, and a wide range of other Chinese imports. Whites and Chinese residents alike frequented Fee Lee's shop. White men were also known to frequent the Chinese gambling halls to play the Chinese Lottery, the forerunner to what is now called keno.

Fee Lee's family in Deadwood, 1894

One of the few white men to establish a good relationship with the Chinese was Sol Star. He was also one of the few white men allowed to participate in meetings at the town's Chinese Masonic Lodge. Star even helped run the Caucasian League and Miners Union out of town when, soon after the organization was created, four Chinese houses were burned down and there was a threat to blow up another one.

When there was no more gold to be mined and Deadwood's economy began to slide, the Chinese started drifting out of Deadwood around 1918. After the federal government passed the Chinese Exclusion Act in 1882 to curtail Chinese immigration, the young Chinese men in America were left with few prospects for finding a wife, and those that were already married were unable to bring their spouses to the U.S. if they had not done so before the law was passed. With dwindling business opportunities and no chance of getting married as long as they were in Deadwood, Chinese immigrants found little reason to stay. By 1935, the Chinese were gone and

Chinatown was a ghost town.

Chapter 8: The Decline and Rebirth of Deadwood

By 1918, the gold rush in Deadwood was over, and the 1920 census showed a 34% drop in Deadwood's official population, dropping it to 2,400 people. Ongoing mining operations continued, but the prospecting days were gone, and as the population declined, so did the economy. The reputation of the Badlands kept tourists away, and even during Prohibition, Deadwood kept up its image because the town virtually ignored the federal ban on alcohol.

The declining population seemed to suggest Deadwood might die out altogether, and this was especially true after another major fire broke out in Deadwood in 1959. Another blow to the town came in 1964 when Interstate 90 passed it by, and another fire in 1987 seemed to be the end for Deadwood at last, despite the fact that the town was a national historic landmark.

However, in a last-ditch effort to save Deadwood, the South Dakota state legislature legalized gambling in Deadwood in 1989. The money made from Deadwood casinos was to go toward revitalizing the town and its historic structures. Ultimately, the gambling saved Deadwood, and today it is a combination of the old and new. Main Street is lined with casinos, one of which is owned by actor Kevin Costner, but it also celebrates its famous past. Plans are even in the works to add entertainment venues to attract national acts. The original residents of Deadwood may not recognize the Deadwood of today, but it is thriving and remains a reminder of an iconic time in the American West.

Online Resources

Other Western history titles by Charles River Editors

Other 19th century history titles by Charles River Editors

Other titles about the West on Amazon

Bibliography

Ames, John. The Real Deadwood. New York: Chamberlain Group. 2004.

Conrad, Jane. "Charles Collins: The Sioux City Promotion of the Black Hills." The South Dakota Historical Society. 1971.
http://www.sdshspress.com/index.php?&id=1405&sub_action=1&afarrzpo=afarrzpo&action=960

Markley, Bill. "Deadwood's Lost Chinatown." *True West Magazine.* May 31, 2006.
http://www.truewestmagazine.com/jcontent/history/history/history-features/5456-deadwoods-

lost-chinatown

Parker, Watson. Deadwood: The Golden Years. Lincoln, NE: University of Nebraska Press. 1981.

Werner, Shawn. "Meet Al Swearengen." *Deadwood Magazine.* August 2009. http://www.deadwoodmagazine.com/article.php?read_id=173

Printed in Great Britain
by Amazon